How to See Jesus

Betty J. Ramsey

TRILOGY CHRISTIAN PUBLISHERS
Tustin, CA

Trilogy Christian Publishers

A Wholly Owned Subsidiary of Trinity Broadcasting Network

2442 Michelle Drive

Tustin, CA 92780

For information, address Trilogy Christian Publishing

Rights Department, 2442 Michelle Drive, Tustin, Ca 92780.

For information about special discounts for bulk purchases, please contact Trilogy Christian Publishing.

Manufactured in the United States of America

10 9 8 7 6 5 4 3 2 1

Library of Congress Cataloging-in-Publication Data is available.

ISBN 978-1-64088-603-2

ISBN 978-1-64088-604-9 (ebook)

Contents

All Scripture Quotes are from the King James Version of the *Holy Bible,* Public Domain.

CHAPTER 1

Who Am I?

"I am the vine, you *are* the branches: He that abides in me, and I in him, the same brings forth much fruit: for without me you can do nothing."
(John 15:5)

"Hitler stood naked in front of the mirror examining his parts..." suggested the professor standing in front of the class of wannabe writers. "You need a hook, a great hook to capture the readers' attention."

He continued his spiel as his every-other-word cursing burned my ears. Inwardly groaning, I wished the clock hands would fly around the clock face so the class would soon be over so I could get some golden silence. This man may have had some intelligence at one time, but he seemed to have lost it as his verbiage was pure gutter curses. Looking around the classroom at the young ears of the college students listening, I wondered if America's colleges and universities only hire the most base and mundane people for professors because they have added writing a book to their resume. When the class was finally over, all his thoughts on his writing process just vanished from my brain until twelve years later when I found my notes in an old notebook and reread them.

Inside this physical body is a spiritual body. A beautiful, young healthy person dressed by God in an ethereal way that seems more real than the body in this world. This spiritual body is a person for His glory. His love. Just as we have this spiritual body so does He, only He can move from one person to another when He wants to show or to see or to do something in the flesh or physical that is in this world. When this saga began, I had no idea that He could do that or the limitations of our earthly flesh. This book is a tiny representation of the things He can do and be while He is hiding in plain sight. My hope is that after reading this book that you will begin to experience an awareness of His presence and that your spiritual eyes will open to the invisible world around you and the kingdom that exists within this physical world.

> In the beginning was the Word, and the Word was with God, and the Word was God. The same was in the beginning with God. All things were made by him; and without him was not any thing made that was made. In him was life; and the life was the light of men. And the light shines in darkness; and the darkness comprehended it not.
>
> John 1:1-5

Continuing with his description of the Word, John says:

> But as many as received him, to them he gave power to become the sons of God, even to them that believe on his name: Which were born, not of blood, nor of the will of the flesh, nor of the will of man, but of God. And the Word was made flesh, and dwelt (lived) among us, (and we beheld his glory, the glory as of the only begotten of the Father,) full of grace and truth.
>
> John 1:12-14

He became a man: mortal, fragile, and subject to the same conditions that we are subject to so that He could understand everything that we go through and when we think that He does not know something about us, just remember that he experienced it all and more in His human body. In addition, He knew and learned everything from the beginning of the world, the sins, the evil, the wars, the good, the bad and the ugly and yet, He was still as John states in John 1:16-18,

> And of his fullness have all we received, and grace for grace. For the law was given by Moses, *but* grace and truth came by Jesus Christ. No man hath seen God at any time; the only begotten Son, which is in the bosom of the Father, he hath declared *him*.

Most pastors quote the "No man hath seen God at any time" taken out of context and leave off that *Jesus Christ has declared Him*.

Robert Jamieson, A.R. Fausset, and David Brown posit that, "No man, no one, in the widest sense. Hath seen God by immediate gaze, or direct intuition."

This is at odds with all the people who say that they have seen Jesus Christ or God. In 1970, I had an out-of-body experience when I died and went to heaven and saw Jesus. His most distinctive features were the most beautiful and loving eyes of all creation. In 2015, I saw those eyes again in Israel. This time not only were they beautiful and loving but they added light beams to them. Those same eyes show up in a photo that I had taken that looks like a gray cloud while I was walking on the first floor of the Church of the Holy Sepulcher. In 2016, they were there again in a different man and they moved out of his eyes by sliding sideways like glass curtains out of view. Then in 2018, I saw them looking at me from around another person with all the beauty and love that eyes could hold in a restaurant of the hotel I stayed in. Dark, sparkling, beautiful eyes not at all like the hazel-colored eyes of the person they were in.

There are many instances of God being in a cloud, in the form of a cloud pillar or speaking from a cloud in the Holy Bible. Exodus, Leviticus, Deuteronomy, 1 Kings, 2 Chronicles, Nehemiah, Job, Psalms, Isaiah, Jeremiah, Lamentation, Ezekiel, Daniel, Hosea, Joel, Nahum, Zechariah, Matthew, Mark, Luke, Acts, 1 Corinthians, 1 Thessalonians, Hebrews, 2 Peter, Jude, and Revelation contain many verses confirming God's existence in some cloud form. One example is Exodus 34:5, "and the LORD descended in the cloud, and stood with him (Moses) there, and proclaimed the name of the LORD."

Jesus told His disciples when the righteous might see Him as He sat on the Mount of Olives and answered their questions on the end times. In Matthew 25:42-46 it states,

> For I was hungry, and you gave me no meat: I was thirsty, and you gave me no drink: I was a stranger, and you took me not in: naked, and you clothed me not: sick, and in prison, and you visited me not. Then shall they also answer him, saying, Lord, when did we see you hungry, or thirsty, or a stranger, or naked, or sick, or in prison, and did not minister unto you? Then shall he answer them, saying, Verily I say unto you, inasmuch as you did it not to one of the least of these, you did *it* not to me. And these shall go away into everlasting punishment: but the righteous into life eternal.

Jesus can appear in any person and in any form He chooses. He gave many examples as *I am* statements in John.

> And Jesus said unto them, I am the bread of life: he that comes to me shall never hunger; and he that believes on me shall never thirst. But I said unto you, That you also have seen me, and believe not.
>
> John 6:35-36

> John 6:51 "I am the living bread which came down from heaven: if any man eats of this bread, he shall live for ever: and the bread that I will give is my flesh, which I

> will give for the life of the world." Then spake Jesus again unto them, saying, I am the light of the world: he that follows me shall not walk in darkness, but shall have the light of life. (John 8:12)xx John 8:18 I am one that bear witness of myself, and the Father that sent me bears witness of me. John 8:58 Jesus said unto them, Verily, verily, I say unto you, Before Abraham was, I am. John 10:7-9 Then said Jesus unto them again, Verily, verily, I say unto you, I am the door of the sheep. All that ever came before me are thieves and robbers: but the sheep did not hear them. I am the door: by me if any man enters in, he shall be saved, and shall go in and out, and find pasture. John 10:14 I am the good shepherd, and know my sheep, and am known of mine. John 14:6 Jesus saith unto him, I am the way, the truth, and the life: no man comes unto the Father, but by me. John 15:1 I am the true vine, and my Father is the husbandman.

Bread has various meanings that can be applied to *I am the bread*. Bread can be dough that when baked and eaten, sustains a person and gives energy. Bread can be money or a livelihood as well. Jesus called Himself bread meaning He can supply all these things including eternal life and He gave His flesh for all of us. He is our light not only to guide and show us the way, but He provides the light of life so that we may live forever with Him. He is the faithful witness of God and He is the door. A great heresy that is being announced is, that there is more than one way to God. But that is not so and a lie that condemns many people to torment. Jesus is the one door and the one way to God the Father. He came as a servant and shepherd and He knows who follows Him and who does not. He is omniscient and omnipotent.

John has other insights in the gospel that provide a picture of who Jesus was, is and how He can do the things He does.

> Then said Jesus again unto them, I go my way, and you shall seek me, and shall die in your sins: where I go, you cannot come. Then said the Jews, Will he kill himself? because he says, Where I go, you cannot come. And he said unto them, You are from beneath; I am from above: you are of this world; I am not of this world.
>
> John 8:21-23

John 8:28-29 Then said Jesus unto them, When you have lifted up the Son of man, then shall you know that I am *he,* and *that* I do nothing of myself; but as my Father has taught me, I speak these things. And he that sent me is with me: the Father has not left me alone; for I do always those things that please him. John 8:56-58 Your father Abraham rejoiced to see my day: and he saw *it,* and was glad. Then said the Jews unto him, You are not yet fifty years old, and have you seen Abraham? Jesus said unto them, Verily, verily, I say unto you, Before Abraham was, I am. John 14:7-11 If you had known me, you should have known my Father also: and from henceforth you know him, and have seen him. Philip said unto him, Lord, shew us the Father, and it suffices us. Jesus said unto him, Have I been so long time with you, and yet have you not known me, Philip? he that has seen me has seen the Father; and how can you say *then,* Shew us the Father? Believe you not that I am in the Father, and the Father in me? the words that I speak unto you I speak not of myself: but the Father that dwells in me, he does the works. Believe me that I *am* in the Father, and the Father in me: or else believe me for the very works' sake.

Even though the disciples had been with Jesus through many experiences, they still found it hard to recognize who He was. It has not changed today because people still have a difficult time recognizing Jesus and seeing Him for who He is.

CHAPTER 2

Hidden

"But as it is written, Eye hath not seen, nor ear heard, neither have entered into the heart of man, the things which God has prepared for them that love him."
(1 Corinthians 2:9)

In 2018, I was on a Lufthansa jet traveling from the USA to Germany and after a few hours, I went to sleep. He awakened me during the night as the jet flew far to the north. I looked out the tiny window at an awesome sight. The Big Dipper was alone in a dark expanse of black sky framed in the window. I excitedly looked around the interior of the jet but everyone was asleep and I turned back to the window amazed at such beauty. What a creator that He could show me His display of seven magnificent stars so close and yet so far away! What an intimate moment with God that I alone saw because He was there to awaken me. Awesome!

> Hast thou not known? hast thou not heard, that the everlasting God, the LORD, the Creator of the ends of the

> earth, faints not, neither is weary? *There* is no searching of his understanding.
> Isaiah 40:28

"I *am* the LORD, your Holy One, the creator of Israel, your King." (Isaiah 43:15)

For Jesus, there was no other way but to do what He did by His sacrifice on the cross. He proved many times that He could escape by being invisible to people. He could make people blind to His physical presence. He could make them forget what was happening and when it happened. He could change His appearance, His clothing (Luke 9:29) and He had the power to call forth legions of angels (Luke 26:53). He is not dead but is truly living! He overcame death to become the living Spirit of God. Open your spiritual eyes and see Jesus, for He is worthy to be seen and experienced in a relationship as a living savior.

Then in John 14:6 "Jesus saith unto him, I am the way, the truth, and the life: no man comes unto the Father, but by me."

Only Jesus can give you rest and peace and love that will fill your heart and soul. Only He can send the Holy Spirit, your comforter from God.

> For I am persuaded, that neither death, nor life, nor angels, nor principalities, nor powers, nor things present, nor things to come, Nor height, nor depth, nor any other creature, shall be able to separate us from the love of God, which is in Christ Jesus our Lord.
>
> Romans 8:38-39

Traveling with my sister, we were blessed to go to Israel with TBN's 2018 Praise & Worship Tour. The Lufthansa jet landed in Tel Aviv and we were taken to our hotel in Jerusalem where we resided the entire tour. It was exciting and wonderful to meet two thousand people and sing and praise God all over Israel with big praise events at the Southern Steps, Galilee, The Garden Tomb, and Caesarea. In addition to the events of praise and worship, there were excursions to the Jordan River Valley, Masada, Megiddo, Jezreel, and many walking tours of Jerusalem.

This was our third tour to Israel and each tour added to the clarity of knowing how to see Jesus.

Those eyes could compel, sparkle and shine with love. I have never seen eyes on earth like those eyes. They had a life of their own. They could look right into your soul and see what was hidden there. They could look into your mind and see what you were thinking. They drew me in like a magnet and looking away was almost impossible, if not impossible. I didn't want to look away...I wanted to enjoy those eyes for as long as I could. I had a supernatural memory of them.

My other senses didn't seem to work during the 2015 or 2016 tour. The group walked over a sewer and I didn't smell it. I don't remember smelling any odors at all but this last trip, I smelled urine on every street we walked down like men had urinated on every wall to make their mark like a dog marking its territory. I could hear sounds of people talking and when He came up to me begging for money, no one seemed to see Him but me. He pushed in front of a man asking to be our guide, seeming to materialize from nowhere. He waved his arms and hands in front of us and jumped up and down. He was wearing what appeared to be a rumpled gray suit. His salt-and-pepper beard made an impression on me and I wanted to reach out and touch it but I didn't.

I reached into my bag and took out some rolled up American dollar bills and His hand was warm on mine as He took the money I handed Him and the feel of His hand remained with me for days. At night, I was asleep and dreaming when I was awakened by a jostling going on in me like a battle. I had an impression of a face with a salt-and-pepper beard and someone holding me. My sister awakened me. I pulled the cover up to my chin.

"What is wrong with you?" she asked.

"I guess it was a nightmare," I replied. I remembered nothing but my dream of rescuing some children from a mudslide at that time.

I asked her, "Why?" She just shook her head and didn't answer, looking puzzled.

Only Jesus knew our seventh-floor room number, but our door was locked and securely dead-bolted from the inside. The balcony was not close to anything and had curved walls on both sides that were not scaleable. Too, there was no one visible to the eyes! But I know He was there!

> Then shall they also answer him, saying, Lord, when saw we thee an hungry, or thirsty, or a stranger, or naked, or sick, or in prison, and did not minister unto thee? Then

> shall he answer them, saying, Verily I say unto you, inasmuch as ye did it not to one of the least of these, ye did it not to me.
>
> Matthew 25:44-45

He was there in Jerusalem but even though His appearance had changed, He was the center and most important part of the tour for me. This time He was dressed as a beggar so you may never know what He will appear as when you visit Israel or what He may say or do. It happened so quickly at Joppa Gate that I had a fleeting memory of the soft beard on His face and the warmth of His hand as I passed some money into His like a baton behind me. Thinking of Matthew 25:44-45, I tried to pass money to every beggar or homeless person I saw on the tour. There was a man with one leg in a wheelchair on the way to Mount Zion, a man bent over in Gethsemane, a lady with no money to use a restroom, a child selling gum in Bethlehem and still others. Were they all Him? Is it necessary to give money to every one of them? I don't know, but I don't want to pass Him up if even one of them is Jesus and I have anything left to give. This wisdom was learned in 2018 from a previous tour.

CHAPTER 3

The Saga Begins

"I have called upon thee, for thou wilt hear me, O God: incline thine ear unto me, and hear my speech."
(Psalm 17:6)

All of this started in 2015, when I went on a belated tour with my sister. We left in the dark but awakened to the bright Middle East sun shining above the airport in Tel Aviv. It was so bright I could not take my sunglasses off at all and see.

God was there! I could feel His presence the moment I stepped off the plane. The air was so thick with that undeniable presence. It permeated my entire being with a joyous homecoming feeling. We hurried through security with passport checks and headed to the baggage claim area to pick up our luggage, then on to the lines where we were checked through the customs lines.

It seemed everyone who had been issued either maroon or gold name tags were congregating together at a central location, so we joined them and stayed there until the guides came to take us to our buses. There they told us to match our name tags to the signs on the bus windshield and load our luggage in that bus for the trip to the hotel in Tiberias at the Sea of Galilee.

What an amazing place! The buses rolled through countryside with planted fields and groves of fruit trees along the Jordan River—not unlike what was back home, but here it seemed new and fresh. It was almost dark when we arrived at the Leonardo Hotel and claimed our rooms. From the balcony, the sunset was gorgeous with colors glimmering over the indigo sea, then changing to steel then charcoal then to black. The balcony faced the Sea of Galilee (or Sea of Tiberias as it is also known) with the Golan Heights just across the sea, where its twinkling lights were coming into view with the deepening of the colors and the black of the nightscape. It was amazingly peaceful and breathtaking, all at the same time.

The beginning of the tour started at eight o'clock the next morning after a delicious breakfast in the hotel and a restful night. Everyone was talkative and ready to go. We were on our way to ride across the Sea of Galilee on a boat. Our guide burst into the lobby of the hotel full of energy and asked if we would please follow him. Bewildered slightly, we followed closely on his heels as he led us down a paved street behind the hotel and through a maze of tiny streets to the shore where a boat was waiting with a smiling captain.

"Okay," I said to the ladies beside me. "Who is going to walk on the water first?"

They all said me in unison.

But the guide looked at me with a stern face and said, "Don't joke."

When all were aboard the open-air boat, the captain set the boat in motion and pulled out into the sea. The flags of each country represented by tour member's countries were presented and their national anthem was played while everyone stood and saluted their flag and sang. Australia, New Zealand, Brittan, United States, Africa, India, and China were among those represented. The largest group of tour members was from the USA.

The leader of the tour group read scriptures and everyone read along with them. He taught a lesson on Luke 22 with a window, mirror, and picture where the window is the deeper meaning of what's happening to the apostles; the mirror is how we are feeling when we read the passage and the picture is the history in AD 30 of how the apostles wrote the message. He asked us to imagine how we are like Peter since only the Holy Spirit gives the mirror. The message was so interesting that the time passed quickly and before we knew it, we were on the far shores near a museum where we disembarked and walked to the doors of the museum. Inside were souvenir shops and artifacts. Moving into a large theater area, we saw a movie called *The Jesus Boat,* a boat that was discovered in the Sea of Galilee dating back to the time that Jesus walked on the earth on these same shores. The guide pointed out features of the boat and how it would have been much larger in the days of the apostles, but weathering had taken much of it away and how in the days of Jesus, the people would have used this boat for fishing and travel on the Sea of Galilee or Sea of Tiberias.

Our buses were waiting on the other side of the museum for us to board to go to another site. On the sidewalk, the guide picked up several small figs from the ground and discussed the fig tree.

The buses took us to the Mount of Beatitudes where our tour leader read the Beatitudes from the scriptures in Matthew 5:3-11 and John 21:1-19 on overcoming fear. When talking about the person Peter, In essence, Jesus looked into Peter's soul and saw his fear. Jesus question was, "Do you love me, Peter?" Jesus wanted the apostles to feed people with His words, the gospel and to follow Him as an example.

Leaving the Mount of Beatitudes, we traveled to the Galilee shores to the Church of the Primacy of Saint Peter on the Galilee. After a short service on the feeding of the five thousand miracle (Mark 6:35-44), most of the tourists waded into the warm water and took photos of the church. This is the place where Jesus fed his disciples breakfast and sat and taught the people. Today, a Catholic church is built around the soil mound believed to be the very spot Jesus sat on.

Boarding the buses again, we arrive at a restaurant for lunch to eat Saint Peter's Fish. As we ate a delicious baked tilapia fish, we talked about Jesus, Peter and His disciples and how this was the fish they might have eaten. Flowering shrubs grew outside the restaurant and the waters of the Galilee could be seen in the distance making an ambient quietness within.

The next stop was in Capernaum and the synagogue there. The scriptures read were Matthew 1:1-6 on the genealogy of Jesus Christ. The Hebrews' description of John the Baptist as Elijah and, "I will raise them up a Prophet from among their brethren, like unto thee, and will put my words in his mouth; and he shall speak unto them all that I shall command him. " Deuteronomy 18:18 "These were the signs we have waited for."

The synagogue on the top layer of stones was Roman architecture but under the top layer was another synagogue and under the previous one was another synagogue in another layer of dark stones that would have been present about the time of Jesus. Much of Jesus' ministry was spent there in Capernaum where Peter's mother-in-law lived.

Luke 4:43-44 says, "And he said unto them, I must preach the kingdom of God to other cities also: for therefore am I sent. And he preached in the synagogues of Galilee."

> And Jesus returned in the power of the Spirit into Galilee: and there went out a fame of him through all the region round about. And he taught in their synagogues,

> being glorified of all. And he came to Nazareth, where he had been brought up: and, as his custom was, he went into the synagogue on the Sabbath day, and stood up for to read. And there was delivered unto him the book of the prophet Esaias. And when he had opened the book, he found the place where it was written, The Spirit of the Lord *is* upon me, because he hath anointed me to preach the gospel to the poor; he hath sent me to heal the brokenhearted, to preach deliverance to the captives, and recovering of sight to the blind, to set at liberty them that are bruised, To preach the acceptable year of the Lord. And he closed the book, and he gave *it* again to the minister, and sat down. And the eyes of all them that were in the synagogue were fastened on him.
>
> Luke 4:14-20

He was Messiah of the Jews and Gentiles, too.

> And he (Jesus) said unto them, you will surely say unto me this proverb, Physician, heal thyself: whatsoever we have heard done in Capernaum, do also here in your country. And he said, Verily I say unto you, No prophet is accepted in his own country. But I tell you of a truth, many widows were in Israel in the days of Elias (Elijah), when the heaven was shut up three years and six months, when great famine was throughout all the land; But unto none of them was Elias sent, save unto Sarepta, *a city* of Sidon, *unto a* woman that was a widow. And many lepers

> were in Israel in the time of Eliseus (Elisha) the prophet; and none of them was cleansed, saving Naaman the Syrian. And all they in the synagogue, when they heard these things, were filled with wrath, And rose up, and thrust him out of the city, and led him unto the brow of the hill whereon their city was built, that they might cast him down headlong. But he passing through the midst of them went his way...
>
> Luke 4:23-30

On the way back to the hotel, the buses took us to the city of Nazareth where Jesus declared His ministry by reading Isaiah 61:1-2 and where we walked up to the top of a hill overlooking the Valley of Jezreel to the precipice. Here the Valley of Jezreel and Nazareth cities meet on the slopes down the hillside and other cities loom around all sides from Mount Tabor on the Plain of Esdraelon to the Nazareth villages. The valley is filled with growing vegetation for food. Strip cropping with bare hay fields and green fields wove a quilt top in many colors. Water resources are scattered here and there to keep the fertile fields growing and green. It was so outstanding and spectacular that when I thought of the destruction forecasted at Armageddon, I prayed so hard for God to spare it and these people who are called the Jews, who have been so abused by mankind that *He answered me back!* I was so shocked and startled when I heard Him and His voice that I stopped praying and thanked Him! He was there! He is there! Thank you, God! You are there!

I didn't have my map with me, but there on that little hill was a sign stating that this was the Mount of Precipice or the Leaping Mountain, 397 meters high with a lookout over Nazareth, Mt. Tabor and the Yizrael Valley at its foot. According to an old tradition, Jesus jumped from the mountain to flee his pursuers. It also states that at the foot of the mountain is the "Oafzer" Cave where Neolithic remains were found about 7,000-10,000 BC in the remains of the Mosterian Period. This is possibly the place mentioned in Luke 4:23-30 where they would have cast Him down the hill but He passed through them and went His way without their seeing Him. Looking down the side of the mountain, it would have been impossible for a normal person to jump off it and not be injured or killed.

In the valley below the hill was the City of Nain, where the woman's son was raised by Jesus from the dead.

> And it came to pass the day after, that he went into a city called Nain; and many of his disciples went with him, and much people. Now when he came nigh to the gate of the city, behold, there was a dead man carried out, the only son of his mother, and she was a widow: and much people of the city was with her. And when the Lord saw her, he had compassion on her, and said unto her, Weep not. And he came and touched the bier: and they that bare *him* stood still. And He said, Young man, I say unto thee, Arise. And he that was dead sat up, and began to speak. And he delivered him to his mother."
>
> Luke 7:11-15

What a miracle!

This is the same place where Barak and Deborah fought a war and won when the Lord discomfited Sisera making it easier for their capture.

> And Deborah said unto Barak, Up; for this *is* the day in which the LORD hath delivered Sisera into thine hand: is not the LORD gone out before thee? So, Barak went down from Mount Tabor and ten thousand men after him. And the LORD discomfited Sisera, and all *his* chariots, and all *his* host, with the edge of the sword before Barak; so that Sisera lighted down off *his* chariot and fled away on his feet.
>
> Judges 4:14-15

Nazareth is the city disparaged by Nathanael from Cana in John 1:46-47.

> And Nathanael said unto him, "Can there any good thing come out of Nazareth?" Philip said unto him, "Come and see." Jesus saw Nathanael coming to him, and said of him, "Behold an Israelite indeed, in whom is no guile!"

Yes, indeed, something very good came out of Nazareth! The divine man, Jesus Christ was born of a virgin and the Holy Ghost and who, as our sacrifice, is our mediator between God and man. The Church of the Annunciation was pointed out to the group, but we did not visit it. According to guides, the church is built over the grotto where Mary lived and was visited by the angel, Gabriel. The church or basilica is operated by the Roman Catholic Church.

> And in the sixth month the angel Gabriel was sent from God unto a city of Galilee, named Nazareth, to a virgin espoused to a man whose name was Joseph, of the house of David; and the virgin's name was Mary. And the angel came in unto her, and said, Hail, thou that art highly favored, the Lord is with thee: blessed art thou among women. And when she saw him, she was troubled at his saying, and cast in her mind what manner of salutation this should be. And the angel said unto her, Fear not, Mary: for you have found favor with God. And, behold, you shalt conceive in thy womb, and bring forth a son, and shalt call his name JESUS. He shall be great and shall be called the Son of the Highest: and the Lord God shall give unto him the throne of his father David: And he shall reign over the house of Jacob forever; and of his kingdom there shall be no end. Then said Mary unto the angel, how shall this be, seeing I know not a man? And the angel answered and said unto her, The Holy Ghost shall come upon thee, and the power of the Highest shall overshadow thee: therefore, also that holy thing which shall be born of thee shall be called the Son of God.
>
> Luke 1:26-35

As we headed back to the buses, shots rang out from Nazareth and a Muslim call sounded from mosque towers. The guide said it wasn't really a prayer they were saying, but more like an advertisement.

> Hear, O my people, and I will testify unto thee: O Israel, if thou wilt hearken unto me; There shall no strange god be in thee; neither shalt thou worship any strange god. I am the LORD thy God, which brought thee out of the land of Egypt: open thy mouth wide, and I will fill it.
>
> Psalm 81:8-10 (KJV)

God is there. His presence is felt on every hill and in every space. From the Church of the Annunciation to the trees with His Spirit moving the leaves, He is there!

"The LORD reigns, he is clothed with majesty; the LORD is clothed with strength, wherewith he hath girded himself: the world also is established, that it cannot be moved" (Psalm 93:1). His presence is there in Israel.

The guide gave us a reading assignment to read about the five women mentioned in Jesus' genealogy. They were Thamor, Rachab, Ruth, Bathsheba, and Mary. Two of these women were Gentiles by birth, Ruth and Rachab, while the others had a blot by their names according to Jewish Law in the Old Testament: Thamor, Rachab, Bathsheba and Mary although she was a virgin, was unwed at the time of her impregnation. These ladies represent the unsearchable riches of God's grace in the genealogy. Praise God!

CHAPTER 4

He is There!

"Praise ye the LORD. Praise God in his sanctuary: praise him in the firmament of his power" (Psalm 150:1)

After a peaceful night's sleep by the Sea of Galilee, the tour set out to the north to Mount Hermon, Dan, and Caesarea Philippi. Our first stop was the Tel Dan Nature Reserve. Trees of many species border the path that leads over the rushing waters from Mount Hermon including imported eucalyptus trees.

> When the poor and needy seek water, and there is none, and their tongue fails for thirst, I the LORD will hear them, I the God of Israel will not forsake them. I will open rivers in high places, and fountains in the midst of the valleys: I will make the wilderness a pool of water, and the dry land springs of water. I will plant in the wilderness the cedar, the shittah tree, and the myrtle, and the oil tree; I will set in the desert the fir tree, and the pine, and the box tree together: That they may see, and

> know, and consider, and understand together, that the hand of the LORD hath done this, and the Holy One of Israel hath created it.
>
> Isaiah 41:17-20

All around was an abundance of trees and water. Praise God forever! Praise His holy name! The guide led the group up a trail to meet the other bus group and join the tour leader for a service beside pools of clear water. The message was Psalm 42:1-11 "As the hart pants after the water brooks, so pants my soul after thee, O God. My soul thirsts for God, for the living God: when shall I come and appear before God? My tears have been my meat day and night, while they continually say unto me, where is thy God? When I remember these things, I pour out my soul in me: for I had gone with the multitude, I went with them to the house of God, with the voice of joy and praise, with a multitude that kept holyday. Why are you cast down, O my soul? and why are you disquieted in me? hope thou in God: for I shall yet praise him for the help of his countenance. O my God, my soul is cast down within me: therefore, will I remember thee from the land of Jordan, and of the Hermonites, from the hill Mizar. Deep calls unto deep at the noise of thy waterspouts: all thy waves and thy billows are gone over me. Yet the LORD will command his loving kindness in the daytime, and in the night his song shall be with me, and my prayer unto the God of my life. I will say unto God my rock, Why hast thou forgotten me? why go I mourning because of the oppression of the enemy? As with a sword in my bones, mine enemies reproach me; while they say daily unto me, Where is thy God? Why art thou cast down, O my soul? and why art thou disquieted within me? hope thou in God: for I shall yet praise him, who is the health of my countenance, and my God."

Nothing can satisfy us but the Lord Jesus Christ! The people of Mount Hermon are mentioned in verse six. The deep calls to the deep, like the sound of waves one after another washing over one. God is our rock and refuge who gives us good health and hope even in struggles when the water seems over our heads. This prayer or testimony of David's praise to God for His divine help is in a time of great trouble and trials.

At the conclusion of the service, the guide led the group up a trail where he pulled some wild rice seed from plants growing by the path and some wild mustard seeds from plants and compares the tiny mustard seed to the rice seed for size just as Jesus did as we made our way to the ancient city of Dan. Dan was the fifth son of Jacob by Bilhah, Rachel's maid which means "God has judged me," in Hebrew, *dananni*. The blessing pronounced on him by his father was that, "Dan shall judge his people" (Gen 49:16). The tribe of Dan had their place in the march through the wilderness on the north side of the tabernacle (Num 2:25, 31; Num 10:25).

It was the last of the tribes to receive a portion in the Promise Land. The territory of Dan was situated between that of Ephraim and Benjamin west of the sea. Although it was not a large territory, it did have fertile soil and included cities like Lydda, Ekron, and Joppa on its northern border. The Amorites and the Philistines were on both sides, and so the at the

Danites were unable to conquer, so that the Danites wanted more land.

They sent out five spies from two of their towns, who went north to the beginning of the Jordan and brought back a favorable report regarding that region. "Arise," they said, "be not slothful to go, and to possess the land, for it is a place where there is no want of anything that is in the earth" (Judges 18:10).

On receiving this report, 600 Danites took up their weapons of war and along with their wives and their children, marched to the foot of Mount Hermon and fought against Leshem and took it from the Sidonians and lived there. They changed the name of the conquered town to Dan (Joshua 19:47). This new city of Dan became to them a new home and was the northern limit of Israel.

The mounds of ruins which mark the site of the city today show that at one time, it covered a considerable amount of ground. This old border city was originally called Lachish. (Judges 18:7 and Isaiah 10:30) A sign is posted so that visitors know about Lachish and archaeological excavations still being performed on it. It was originally occupied during the Neolithic Period, circa 4500 BC although during the fourth millennium, it was abandoned for one thousand years and was covered with soil and grasses. Stones and artifacts found there match 2 Samuel 19:8 that states,

> Then the king arose and sat in the gate. And they told unto all the people, saying, Behold, the king doth sit in

> the gate. And all the people came before the king: for Israel had fled every man to his tent.

The walls of the city buildings are without mortar but have small stones used to level and prop large stones in place. The streets are paved with flat or nearly flat, worn stones. Around and up a hill stands King Jeroboam's altar where he set up golden calves to be worshiped as gods.

> Whereupon the king took counsel, and made two calves of gold, and said unto them, It is too much for you to go up to Jerusalem: behold thy gods, O Israel, which brought thee up out of the land of Egypt. And he set the one in Bethel, and the other put he in Dan. And this thing became a sin: for the people went to worship before the one, even unto Dan. And he made an house of high places, and made priests of the lowest of the people, which were not of the sons of Levi.
>
> 1 Kings 12:28-31

King Jeroboam became known as the man, "who made Israel to sin." The remains of the idolatrous altar are still there, pointing to his legacy buried under dirt and grass.

Along the same trail, just past a demilitarized zone that neither Israel nor Lebanon can use, is a city in Lebanon with Mount Hermon serenely in sight. Another site under archaeological excavation is deemed to be "Abraham's Gate." Covered by an elaborate modern roof structure for protection against the elements, it shows a gate filled with soil and a building just emerging from the hill it is buried under. The walls appear to be mud bricks on top of a stone foundation. Stones were used as pavers for the street up to the gate. Tarps cover much of the dig to protect it from rain but there is a lot still visible. A model of the proposed site and benches for tourists are arranged in front of the display.

> And he said, Take now thy son, thine only son Isaac, whom thou lovest, and get thee into the land of Moriah; and offer him there for a burnt offering upon one of the mountains which I will tell thee of. And Abraham called the name of that place Jehovah Jireh: as it is said to this day, In the mount of the LORD it shall be seen.
>
> Genesis 22:14

Where ever that mountain was, it took Abraham at least three days to get there from where he was living. God told Abraham *He* would tell him which mountain to go to but he did not reveal it to us. Many say it was Jerusalem. Some say it was Hermon.

Dan is about four miles away from Caesarea Philippi, in the midst of a region of unsurpassing richness and beauty. Caesarea Philippi is a city on the northeast of the marshy plain of el-Huleh, 120 miles north of Jerusalem, and twenty miles north of the Sea of Galilee near the base of Mount Hermon at the beginning source of the Jordan. It is mentioned in Matthew 16:13 and Mark 8:27 as the most northern place of Jesus' public ministry. According to some, its original name was Baal-Gad (Joshua 11:17) or Baal-Hermon (Judges 3:3; 1 Chronicles 5:23) when it was a Canaanite sanctuary for the worship of idol god Baal. It was afterwards called Panium or Paneas from a deep cavern full of water near the town.

This name was given to the cavern by the Greeks of the Macedonian kingdom of Antioch because of its likeness to the grottos of Greece, which were associated with the worship of their god Pan. Its modern name is Baniass. Here Herod built a temple, which he dedicated to Augustus Caesar. This town was enlarged and embellished by Herod Philip, the tetrarch of Trachonitis. His territory included this place, and was called by Caesarea Philippi, partly after his own name and partly after that of the emperor Tiberius Caesar. This name distinguishes it from Caesarea Maritima, the port city.

The pock-marked sides of the hill have niches carved into them for the placement of idols of these gods. Some held tiny figurines while others almost life-sized statues. The hill has cracks and fissures in the rock formations that look as though they could break and fall in a landslide at any moment. From the foundations and the columns lying in ruins, it is easy to see that there was a time when this was all a very elaborate spa area for pagan worship. Although dry of water now, the grotto was once used to sacrifice children and adults by drowning them there in a pagan cult in the third century BC of the Romans and Greeks. One sign says that, "The ritual sacrifices were cast into a natural abyss reaching the underground waters at the back of a cave. If the victims disappeared in the water, this was a sign that the god had accepted the offering. If however; signs of blood appeared in the nearby springs, it meant the sacrifice had been rejected."

I thank God that all this madness is gone from this place today.

> When Jesus came into the coasts of Caesarea Philippi, he asked his disciples, saying, Whom do men say that I

> the Son of man am? And they said, Some say that thou art John the Baptist: some, Elias; and others, Jeremias, or one of the prophets. He said unto them, But whom say ye that I am? And Simon Peter answered and said, Thou art the Christ, the Son of the living God. And Jesus answered and said unto him, Blessed art thou, Simon Barjona: for flesh and blood hath not revealed it unto thee, but my Father which is in heaven. And I say also unto thee, That thou art Peter, and upon this rock I will build my church; and the gates of hell shall not prevail against it. And I will give unto thee the keys of the kingdom of heaven: and whatsoever thou shalt bind on earth shall be bound in heaven: and whatsoever thou shalt loose on earth shall be loosed in heaven. Then charged he his disciples that they should tell no man that he was Jesus the Christ.
>
> Matthew 16:13-20

Jesus' ministry would have been a stark and quiet comparison to what was going on at Caesarea Philippi with the sacrifices to gods in the grotto of Pan and the sexual sins participated in by the proponents of Baal worshipers, Zeus and of course, Nemesis, the goddess of vengeance.

Hermon River Springs flows from underneath the hillside where Caesarea Philippi is located. It is a quiet and peaceful place that has souvenir shops and a restaurant where we could sit by the springs, eat lunch, and share fellowship and reflections. After lunch, the tour turned toward Mount Hermon and the surrounding countryside was filled with scenes of farming and orchards with fruit trees. Crossing over many hills, the guide pointed out a castle on a hill near Damascus, Syria. Rows of fruit trees dotted the landscape as the bus traveled upward. Villages under new construction appeared on the scene.

Near Mount Bental, pieces of equipment from the Six Day War were turned into works of art after the conclusion of the 1967 Six Day War with tank and gun parts made into sculptures. At an amazing observatory, glimpses of Lebanon and Syria could be seen. A bomb exploded in war-torn Damascus while blue uniformed UN soldiers watched through telescopes from the safety of the pinnacle. No one seemed too excited about the devastation being wrought in the city. (A prelude to the refuge crisis?) After a thorough explanation and historical description of the area, the guide led the tour group back to the buses and on to Lebanon, to the Tamar Halabi restaurant where we ate authentic Druze food of chicken, falafel, and salad.

The Druze live in Northern Israel, Lebanon and Syria. Israel has worked to provide utility networks to their villages, updated their healthcare and provided initiatives to boost student achievement to their mainstreamed students. The Druze are neither Jewish, Christian or Muslim but have their own monotheistic religion as a unique and ethnic group of people. Their culture is Arab and their language is Arabic but since 1948, they have served with Israel Defense Forces and Border Police. Within Israel, they may attain high-level positions in political, military, and public offices. The largest Druze town in Israel is located on Mount Carmel at Daliyat el-Carmel and in Isfiya, also on Mount Carmel.

Back over the Golan Heights the bus descended once again to the Galilee region where the Gadarenes mentioned in Luke 8:26-33 was located.

> And they arrived at the country of the Gadarenes, which is over against Galilee. And when he went forth to land, there met him out of the city a certain man, which had devils long time, and wore no clothes, neither abode in any house, but in the tombs. When he saw Jesus, he cried out, and fell down before him, and with a loud voice said, What have I to do with thee, Jesus, thou Son of God most high? I beseech thee, torment me not. (For he had commanded the unclean spirit to come out of the man. For oftentimes it had caught him: and he was kept bound with chains and in fetters; and he broke the bands, and was driven of the devil into the wilderness.) And Jesus asked him, saying, What is thy name? And he said, Legion: because many devils were entered into him. And they besought him that he would not command them to go out into the deep. And there was there a herd of many swine feeding on the mountain: and they besought him that he would suffer them to enter into them. And he suffered them. Then went the devils out of the man, and entered into the swine and the herd ran violently down a steep place into the lake, and were choked. When they that fed them saw what was done, they fled, and went

> and told it in the city and in the country. Then they went out to see what was done; and came to Jesus, and found the man, out of whom the devils were departed, sitting at the feet of Jesus, clothed, and in his right mind: and they were afraid.

The tour bus stopped at the only place on the Galilee where there was a steep hill that could have been the place mentioned in Luke and allowed everyone to read the scriptures and to take photos of the surrounding countryside. It was almost exactly opposite of the Galilee to where the hotel was located.

CHAPTER 5

Always Listening

"Who is like unto thee, O LORD, among the gods? who is like thee, glorious in holiness, fearful in praises, doing wonders?" (Exodus 15:11)

After another restful night, everyone was ready for new adventures. This was the last day in the Galilee area and there were many sites to visit. The bus started out on the *Via Maris* or the "Way of the Sea," the main road that traverses the Jezreel Valley and goes north toward Damascus, past Mount Tabor with the Arab villages of Daburiyya, Shibli, and Umm al-Ghanam located at its base. Mount Tabor is known to Christians as the Mount of Transfiguration, although other sites like Mount Hermon and the Mount of Olives have also been suggested as the site.

From the Via Maris, one can see the Roman Catholic Church and the Greek Eastern Orthodox Church and Monastery on the top of the mountain. Other structures are visible as well, but the bus keeps rolling toward Tel Megiddo. Starting with a model of the Tel in the Megiddo Museum and Gift Shop, the guide describes the excavations and the artifacts that have been found at each layer of the Tel. Tel Megiddo is a hill composed of twenty-six layers of ruins from different settlements. Its strategic location gives it a view of the Jezreel Valley. Along the top layer, complex concrete block stables are visible with feeding trough artifacts that are suggested to be from King Solomon's era of his chariot cities. Each stable could hold about fifteen horses.

The tour members from both buses gather under a pavilion where scriptures were read at pertaining to Megiddo Joshua 12.

> And these are the kings of the country which Joshua and the children of Israel smote on this side Jordan on the west, from Baalgad in the valley of Lebanon even unto the mount Halak, that goeth up to Seir; which Joshua gave unto the tribes of Israel for a possession according to their divisions...the king of Taanach, one; the king of Megiddo, one; The king of Kedesh, one; the king of Jokneam of Carmel, one; The king of Dor in the coast of

The sun beats down with a relentless heat and one member of the other bus group faints and has to be taken in for a checkup. Meanwhile, the others follow the guide to a storage pit for grain that goes deep into the ground with tiny steps leading down into it. Archaeologists found grain in the bin and identified it as a storage pit for grain possibly for feeding the horses in the stables belonging to Solomon. Following the guide, most of the tour continues to another aspect of the Tel that leads deep underground. A hewn out rock cistern for water has a 115-foot shaft down 186 narrow steps leading to a horizontal tunnel that goes to a pool of water. There is a bridge constructed over the pool for visitors to walk on for another 330 feet that leads to our buses.

Pointing out Mount Carmel across the Jezreel Valley, the bus driver heads the bus in that direction. The bus ascends the steep incline to Mount Carmel after passing long fields of mown and baled hay, fields of sunflowers, and finally forests with cattle grazing under the trees. The bus arrives at a parking lot near a church with a cross on top of its steeple and the guide says that it is the St. Elyas (Elijah) Church. This church is run by the Carmelites, an order of monks of the Catholic Church. From inside, the beautiful strains of an African gospel hymn can be heard. The guide leads us out onto the roof to a spectacular panoramic view of the Jezreel Valley. After a brief history lesson on the area, the group goes down to a pavilion where one of the group leads the prayer and the scripture that mentions Mount Carmel was read from verses in 1 Kings 18:17-46.

Baal pagan worship was considered sexual abuse. King Ahab and his queen Jezebel killed any prophets that spoke against their Baal religion. The books of Judges, Samuel, and Kings, show synchronism by presenting a chronological picture of people fighting immorality, idol worship, and sexual abuse and impurity, some of the same evil spiritual issues facing every nation and society on earth today. A huge statue of Elijah wielding a sword with his foot on one of the Baal prophets stands in front of the church and there are several pavilions with many different groups of people were praying, singing, or reading scripture scattered throughout the courtyard.

Even though I had seen photos of this structure, nothing prepared me for the sight of the aqueduct. It was extensive! A looming, monstrosity of antiquity that stretched northward as far as I could see. Near Caesarea Maritima, the Roman aqueduct was built somewhere around 22 BC, commissioned by King Herod who wanted a reliable source of fresh water delivered from Mount Carmel about sixteen miles away to his castle. Then a second aqueduct was attached to the first by the Legions of Emperor Hadrian about the second century AD that brought water from the Tanninim or Crocodile River and doubled the aqueduct's capacity. This construction was maintained and supplied water for about 1,200 years until the Crusaders added a smaller canal to replace the other two that are still visible today. Although the structure is now only a tourist attraction, it has fallen into disrepair in places despite attempts to keep it maintained. Places where plaster has fallen shows the process the Romans used in constructing the aqueduct using stones, mortar, and various techniques to make an original water-tight structure. This structure is within 500 feet of the Mediterranean Sea with a beach where tourists and locals enjoy the sand and the water. People picnic on both sides of the Roman aqueduct. Many of the group waded into the Mediterranean Sea.

A short distance from the Aqueduct are the remains of a once bustling seaport, Caesarea Maritima, built by Herod the Great about 10 BC. It was built on an older town called "Strato's Tower" and named after Augustus Caesar. It was the capital of the Roman providence, the seat of governors and a headquarters for the Roman troops. It had a spacious artificial harbor and was complete with many buildings of great splendor including Herod's palace with a freshwater swimming pool. There were amphitheaters, the Hippodrome with racing facilities, citadels, and buildings reflecting Roman architecture of the West. It was here that Cornelius the Roman centurion was converted by Peter in Acts 10.

Phillip the evangelist lived in Caesarea Maritima with his four daughters who were prophetesses. (Acts 21:8) From this place Paul also sailed to Tarsus and it was here that he landed when he returned from his second missionary journey.

> And he spake boldly in the name of the Lord Jesus, and disputed against the Grecians: but they went about to

> slay him. Which when the brethren knew, they brought him down to Caesarea, and sent him forth to Tarsus.
>
> Acts 9:29-30

It was in this Caesarea when games were celebrated in the theater in honor of Emperor Claudius, that the King Herod Agrippa I appeared among the people in his theater box dressed in great splendor and in the middle of an idolatrous homage paid to him by the people, was suddenly struck by an angel. He was eaten of worms and perished by the same disease as that of his grandfather, Herod the Great.

> And upon a set day Herod, arrayed in royal apparel, sat upon his throne, and made an oration unto them. And the people gave a shout, saying, "It is the voice of a god, and not of a man." And immediately the angel of the Lord smote him, because he gave not God the glory: and he was eaten of worms and gave up the ghost. But the word of God grew and multiplied.
>
> Acts 12:21-24

Although under reconstruction, all that remains of the theater are rows of seats, the orchestra pit, the stage and entryway arches. Exterior walls and the seating area have been restored to hold about 4,000 spectators. Before his death, King Herod the Great, with the assistance of the Romans, turned this small Phoenician port city into a bustling trade center for maritime trade. In the courtyard of Herod's long-gone palace is an unknown sarcophagus, pieces of massive columns scattered around and the ruins of a freshwater swimming pool complex reaching into the Mediterranean Sea. Our guide points out a visible part of the wall of the eastern wing, the dining area, central hall and two small rooms on each side with visible patterns of intricately laid tiles on these floors of antiquity.

Paul concluded his third missionary journey here when he visits the church as Acts 18:22 says, "And when he had landed at Caesarea, and gone up, and saluted the church, he went down to Antioch." And it was here the prophet Agabus foretold through the Holy Spirit that Paul would be arrested and turned over to the authorities in Jerusalem. (Acts 21:10-11) And in AD 58, Paul was accused of starting a riot in Jerusalem and was sent to Caesarea to be tried by the governor Felix (Acts 25:12-27).

According to our guide, the rows of ancient blocks arranged in rectangles are all that remain of the rooms in Herod's judgment hall where Paul awaited his trial and appealed to Caesar before Festus there. However, being a Roman, Paul demanded to be tried by the emperor in Rome. After his trial in Caesarea Maritima, Paul sails for Rome (Acts 23:23-26; 32) where he is convicted and sometime later executed around AD 67.

The Hippodrome, built by Herod, is identified by the guide and could hold 20,000 spectators for chariot races beside the sea. This is the site used in the filming of the movie *Ben Hur.* With all the ruins of columns, steps, and other artifacts scattered about in the hot sun, the tour concludes, and we board the buses to go toward Jerusalem.

The route to Jerusalem is a marked contrast between modern hotel, business buildings construction, and shepherds tending flocks of sheep beside the highway. Cars and trucks zing by on the interstate highway. If I didn't know I was in Israel, it could be any US city or countryside. The bus acoustics come alive with a rendition of "The Holy City" and everyone joins in to sing, "Jerusalem! Jerusalem! Lift your gates and sing, Hosanna in the highest! Hosanna to your king!"

Winding through two-lane modern streets, we eventually arrived at Mount Scopus. Our guide informs us that this is the place where in days past, the Jews could "scope" out the city without being observed by its residents. After disembarking the buses on Mount Scopus, the guides welcomed us and passed out salted bread and sparkling grape juice for a traditional Salt Covenant from Numbers 18:19.

> All the heave offerings of the holy things, which the children of Israel offer unto the LORD, have I given thee, and thy sons and thy daughters with thee, by a statute forever: it is a covenant of salt for ever before the LORD unto thee and to thy seed with thee.

The preservative property of salt, which keeps meat from spoiling, seems to be an emblem of holiness and permanence. The eating of salt is a pledge of fidelity, binding those involved in a covenant of friendship.

This was our first glimpse of the buildings, walls and the gates of Jerusalem. New buildings, hotels, houses and sky-scrapers in white were everywhere: New Jerusalem.

It was astounding! How could New Jerusalem be built there now? After time for prayer, the buses are reloaded and taken to the hotels. What a marvelous day to arrive in Jerusalem, God's holy city! Praise His name forever!

CHAPTER 6

His Spirit

After a peaceful night and delicious breakfast, the buses take us to the Mount of Olives where we disembark on the top of the hill. The entire group is herded together for a group photo while the photographer hangs onto a strong metal fence on the hillside. A camel walked by and a man leading a camel shouted out, "Camel rides!" A stooped man walks by with his hand out begging for dollars. The group is once again urged to take a seat at an amphitheater straight across from the golden dome of the mosque on the temple mount. The sky is blue and there is Jerusalem shining in all its splendor!

The guide said the crane was the state bird because there were so many around the skyline on new buildings going up. Mount Zion was beside Jerusalem on the south along with the City of David, and a new archaeological dig as well. There were also some specific points of interests to visit like St. Peter's Church of Galicantu. To the west was New Jerusalem with all those terrific white buildings that went on across the skyline and disappeared out of sight.

Cemeteries were built in front of the walls and in front of the Golden Gate or Eastern Gate that started on the Mount of Olives and went down the hill across the Kidron Valley and right to the walls. Our tour leader used Mathew 26 and discussed the events leading up to the crucifixion: Jesus crying for the people of Jerusalem, His preaching at the temple, the fig theory or Jesus' cursing of the fig tree, Passover and His prayers in Gethsemane.

The guide leads our group around the Mount of Olives to the Church of Necropolis where there are small boxes underneath the church called bone boxes. Some of the boxes are decorated but most are plain and look very old. The Church of Pater Noster is a Roman Catholic church there that stands on the traditional site where Jesus taught the Lord's Prayer (Luke 11:2-40). The modern church is built on the site of a fourth century basilica designed by Constantine I to commemorate the Ascension of Jesus Christ.

We move on to the next church shaped like a tear drop. It is the Church of Dominus Flevit, the Latin translation for "The Lord wept." The shape is to symbolize the tears of Christ. According to Luke 19:38-44, the disciples said,

> Blessed be the King that cometh in the name of the Lord: peace in heaven, and glory in the highest. And some of the Pharisees from among the multitude said unto him, Master, rebuke your disciples. And he answered and said unto them, I tell you that, if these should hold their peace, the stones would immediately cry out. And when he was come near, he beheld the city, and wept over it, Saying, If thou had known, even thou, at least in this thy

> day, the things which belong unto thy peace! but now they are hid from thine eyes. For the days shall come upon thee, that thine enemies shall cast a trench about thee, and compass thee round, and keep thee in on every side, And shall lay thee even with the ground, and thy children within thee; and they shall not leave in thee one stone upon another; because thou knew not the time of thy visitation.

Predicting Jerusalem's destruction and the diaspora of the Jewish people, Jesus weeps openly in what is known in Latin as *Flevit super Illam*. And in 70 AD, His prophecy came true just as He said.

Passing by the cemeteries and churches and moving on down the side of the Mount of Olives on a narrow-paved street, we were guided to the Garden of Gethsemane. Ancient olive trees grow in the garden with paths and benches that are used by visitors to say their prayers on. Olive trees get hollow as they age so that the rings cannot be counted even though they continue to grow. Carbon dating was done on one that broke and fell and the carbon dating set its age to over 2,000 years old—before the time of Jesus Christ. How many prayers have been prayed in this place? How many tears wept?

> When Jesus had spoken these words, he went forth with his disciples over the brook Cedron, where was a garden, into which he entered, and his disciples. And Judas also, which betrayed him, knew the place: for Jesus of-

> ten times resorted thither with his disciples. Judas then, having received a band of men and officers from the chief priests and Pharisees, cometh thither with lanterns and torches and weapons. Jesus therefore, knowing all things that should come upon him, went forth, and said unto them, Whom seek ye? They answered him, Jesus of Nazareth. Jesus saith unto them, I am he. And Judas also, which betrayed him, stood with them. As soon then as he had said unto them, I am he, they went backward, and fell to the ground.
>
> John 18:1-6

Amazingly, He did not use His cloak of invisibility or His power to escape what was to come but surrendered to it. He had committed His will to that of His father and nothing could change it. Not Jews nor Gentiles nor any other could stop Him from His sacrifice.

The Franciscans manage the Garden of Gethsemane which was purchased by three Croatians Paul, Anthony and James, Christians from the Sarajevo Knights of the Holy Sepulchre of Jerusalem in 1681 according to a copper colored sign posted on the wall of the garden. Paths lead through the garden with flowers planted throughout in full bloom. A splendid variety of blooms and such blessed peace were in the garden.

We moved along a path and came to the Church of All Nations or Basilica of Gethsemane which is located across the Kidron, the streets and the Eastern Gate or Golden Gate. Inside the church are vaulted ceilings, artworks of scenes of Jesus and white crosses in windows constructed of red glass tiles. Pews for worshipers are aligned with a lectern and a remarkable pipe organ in front of a painting representing Christ praying in Gethsemane with an angel watching over Him. Those who wished to sit and pray or just hang out and reflect were allowed the time to do so.

The walls of Jerusalem grew closer as the group ascended a steep hill on foot to reach the Lion's Gate, or in ancient days, the Sheep's Gate. Walking from the Church of All Nations, across the Kidron Valley Street, and up the hill to the gate reminds us that this is the way that Jesus walked from Gethsemane to Jerusalem. Once again, the guide leads the group like a good shepherd, and we follow him to the Pool of Bethesda. There in ruins are several large columns, broken stone steps leading into the pools and ancient artifacts scattered around the pool. The scriptures read were from John 5.We walked on to the Church of Saint Anne in search of the Upper Room.

The acoustics in the Upper Room were outstanding! The entire tour filled the pews in the room and the tour leader lead the group in two songs. Even though most had never sung together before, it was beautiful. The high-vaulted ceiling rang with the sounds.

Although this is not the original Upper Room, this one had been prepared so that you could see what it could have been like. A table with a linen cloth was set in the center of the room on an area like a stage above some steps and was roped off, similar to reserved space in a restaurant. There was enough room that a large crowd could fill the remaining space.

Next on the tour map is the Via Dolorosa where Jesus Christ carried the cross through the streets of Jerusalem on this street, although the original one is about twenty feet down beneath the present streets. Everyone was both sad and excited as they begin the journey down the worn cobblestone streets. Both sides of the street were filled with shops and merchandise as vendors stood ready to sell their wares. Cars shared the street with tourists who walked quickly to the side to allow them to pass by. Tunnels gave inadequate shade on this hot sunny day. The guide who seemed to be sprinting ahead, stopped suddenly at the *Ecce Homo Arch*, allowing time for everyone to catch up to the group. Above the street is the *Ecce Homo Arch* which in Latin means, "Behold the man."

In John 19:5 it says, "Then came Jesus forth, wearing the crown of thorns, and the purple robe. And Pilate saith unto them, Behold the man!"

These were the words uttered by Pilate, the Roman Procurator, just before sentencing Jesus. The guide adds that the arch was built in the second century BC during the time of the Emperor Hadrian as the entrance gate leading to the Roman Forum or public square. On either side were two smaller arches with the northernmost small arch integrated into the Ecce Homo Basilica.

The guide points out the remnants that remain of the Antonio Fortress, the Roman Fort in the time of Jesus. This fortress in Jerusalem, at the northwest corner of the temple area had gotten its nickname of "the castle" because of its use by the prisoners, including Paul the Apostle. It was from the stairs of this "castle" Paul delivered his famous speech to the multitude in the area below (Acts 21: 34-40). At one time, it was a place where the vestments of the high priest were stored, but Herod fortified it and called it Antonia in honor of his friend Mark Antony.

It was of such great size that it dominated the temple and the Romans chose it for their headquarters, barracks for their army legions and a fort. Although unseen today, it was built on a plateau of rock, separated on the north from the hill by a monstrous ditch. Visible today is a sign with the words, "Antonia Fortress," located above some massive blocks of stone along the walls on the Via Dolorosa. Prayer shawls for sale swayed in the breeze on a restaurant porch near the sign.

Suddenly, the guide turned down some stairs and we followed him underground by the Way of the Nuns. It is cooler here and everyone claimed a bench or a place to sit and the tour leader joined us to read scripture and lead a prayer.

Leaving the cool underground behind, we emerged on the Armenian streets where more shops lined the sides of the Via Dolorosa. The Armenian Catholic Patriarchate announces the third station on the Way of the Cross. Shopping continued on all sides of the street. A sign read, "Coptic Orthodox Patriarchate, Jerusalem St. Anthony Coptic Monastery AD 325" on a church building, blending ancient with modern shoppers. Still another church sign read, "St. Helen's Coptic Church, Station No. 9" above a wooden cross leaning against a stone wall. Located between two stone church walls separated by an arch is a large banner with the orange jumpsuit figures of the Christians that were beheaded in Libya by ISIS. Verses from the Bible are printed across their figures and one read, "They shall put you out of the synagogues: yes, the time comes, that whosoever kills you will think that he offers God service." (John 16:2) Another was Psalm 142:6, "Attend unto my cry; for I am brought very low: deliver me from my persecutors; for they are stronger than I." A picture of Jesus Christ on the cross was looking down above the figures. It was a sad moment for everyone.

Following along behind the guide, we came to a stop at some buildings that appeared to be the rooftop of some buildings. We wait to follow crowds of people on the same journey into the courtyard of the Church of the Holy Sepulcher. This is it! The last four or five stations of the Via Dolorosa on Golgotha, the Place of the Skull, Calvary and the empty Tomb of Jesus Christ are all in this church!

The Church of the Holy Sepulcher was a huge edifice of stone blocks. The arches over the doors have intricate patterns and tall, decorated columns: three on one side and seven in the middle hold the arches. The guide stopped to tell the history of the church and that it was built in AD 325 by Constantine the Great and his mother Helena. However, the church has been rebuilt many times after numerous attempts to destroy it. Since 1854, the structure's appearance has hardly changed, although a small ladder below the top right window called "The Immovable Ladder" has remained there because of a disagreement over which of the many Christian groups was to move it.

The guide turned right toward some steps going into a small arch on the wall just inside the main doors. Another member of the tour, a woman wearing white capri pants and sunglasses and a hat pulled down over her hair followed behind him. They moved quite fast. The steps were steep and narrow. I followed.

I thought to myself, *More steps? How many more steps do we have to climb?*

The backpack was getting heavier on my back as I climbed each step like it now weighed a ton. Out of breath but following closely behind the woman in front of me, I reached the top of the stairs and turned left following the woman.

I heard the voice of the guide, "Ladies. Take off your sunglasses so you can see."

The woman, wearing sunglasses and a hat pulled down over her eyes, didn't even hesitate but kept on going along the worn stone path, across the small hill, and turned to go down some stairs in front of her.

"Take off your sunglasses so you can see," the guide said again as he had stopped in a cul-de-sac hill of white worn stone.

Suddenly in an argumentative mood, I stopped.

"I can't see without my glasses," I said.

"Take off your sunglasses and look at me," the guide commanded.

Again, I argued. "Okay. I can see with my glasses on, but it is not a good idea to take them off."

"Apparently you can't see anything," the guide said.

The thought went through my mind that I was in a foreign country and since he was in the military, he could probably have me deported if I did not follow his orders. I snatched my sunglasses off and looked at him.

He had taken off his own sunglasses and they were on top of his black hair. His red tour cap and water bottle were hanging on his belt. He was looking around at the lights shining from many brilliant chandeliers. Somewhere I heard three distinct voices. A woman's voice sneered derisively, "She is a virgin." One, a man's voice, said as he laughed, "And he is just an innocent Jewish boy." A different man's voice sounded an alarm, "No-o!"

Then as he looked into my eyes, my eyes opened wide to receive the light beams coming from his and at the same time from somewhere above, a burst of bright light like lightning passed from behind the left side of my head. It hit between us with the force of a terrific lightning bolt, but I could not see him anymore because of the vision appearing between us.

A golden, crystal cylinder shape blocked my view of the guide just as my eyes connected with his. I could hear sounds from the guide, but I could not see him at all.

The cylinder was like the revolving doors that mark the entrance to many classic hotels. Framed in gold with clear crystal sides, this golden clear crystal cylinder reached from the spot where we were standing on the rock into the sky like the vortex to a crystal tornado getting smaller as it disappeared out of sight upward. Men in black suits, white shirts and black hats came running up the steps, along the stone path, and into the cylinder and disappeared out of my sight upward. The cylinder was like a clear elevator but with invisible stairs. The men ran into it, then ran diagonally up and around the sides like there were stairs.

I was so amazed that I just stood and gazed up at them. How long this went on, I don't know. Time seemed to stop and stand still while only they were in motion. After some time, they began to whirl around in the sides of the cylinder, changing shapes, coming closer together, distorted and whirling even faster like they were in a blender as they flew up the vortex into the sky toward heaven. *So, this is the way that Jesus came to make for us here on this rock*, the thought went through my mind.

I wanted to see more and struggled to maintain contact with the vision, but the guide's voice interrupted, "You can put your glasses back on," he said.

I put my sunglasses back on and the vision was gone and along with it my memory of it. My mind was empty of memories of anything at all. I could see the guide standing there.

"What is this place?" I asked not knowing where I was.

He looked stunned that I did not know but said, "Some call it The Place of the Skull."

"Then I must go to it." I said as I turned completely around and even though I had no thought as to why or where I was going, I went to the line of people looking at what appeared to be a hole in the floor. The last I saw of the guide, he had turned to the wall, put his arms up in the air, was looking upward and shaking his head.

The lights were bright from candles standing in the sand in a container and brightly lit red and gold chandeliers swung from the ceiling of the room. Icons dazzled in their brilliance behind the people as the light struck them. Finally, my turn came, and I placed my left hand down in the hole in the floor.

A thought went through my brain that it felt like soapstone or the soft, satiny skin on the back of someone's hand. I slowly pulled my left hand from the hole in the floor and my left hand started to tremble and then to shake violently.

Not knowing what was going on or what might happen, the thought came to me that I might faint, so I turned around and hurried to the left and down the stairs in the direction the people in front of me had gone. At the foot of the stairs, I saw the woman I had been following up the stairs leaning against the wall seeming oblivious to anyone or anything around her with her hat pulled down over her face. She did not move. I stepped to the bottom step and noticed I still had my camera in my right hand.

Suddenly, a soft sound behind me made me look up at the top of the stairs and what appeared to be a beautiful man made of sparkling, shiny cloud was looking at me with beautiful brown eyes and smiling the most loving smile. He was coming toward me down the stairs but as I took another step away, he leaped from the second step from the top, changed into something like a flying fleece blanket, spread out and covered me. It entered at my neck and felt like putting on a soft coat on the outside, but this soft fleece coat went on the inside and down inside my body. I struggled to walk toward the back of the church, past the Sanctuary of Adam, as my body felt like it was contorting and something was moving down inside me between my skin and organs, down into my leg muscles and finally stopping at my waist. Words came into my mind, "Resist not the Holy Spirit."

So I tried to relax and just see what was going to happen to me. At that point, things started happening fast in earth time but slow in heaven time. The camera in my hand continued to take photos but my mind does not remember seeing the images in them.

Memories of what happened in the space of a few minutes here evade my mind even though it felt glorious. Then I was standing looking at the mural on the wall of the body of Jesus after the crucifixion. All I could think was, "Wow, wow! Oh, wow!" while sensation after sensation pulsed through my mind and brain. I tried so hard to get my body and mind back under my control! I felt twenty years younger, totally healthy and not a care in the world. Rejuvenated! Renewed! Revived!

Finally, the movements within me had stopped. Closing my eyes and taking deep gulps of air helped to ease the wonderful sensations. People were talking around me. I looked up the stairs and my sister called my name. I could hear the guide speak into the earpiece I placed in my ear.

"We will meet over here," he said.

My sister's voice answered and said, "Some of the others are down the stairs on the first floor."

"Okay, change of plans," said the guide. "We will meet down there."

The group began to descend the stairs. The large mural of the burial of Jesus or Yeshua was on the wall behind me so I moved far enough away from it so I could give the group room to move in to see it. The guide started explaining about the mural, who painted it and how long it had been there. Taking a photo of it and other interesting things in the room helped me to recover somewhat and regain my composure even though I was still in shock and awe.

There was the Stone of Unction where the women who loved Him covered Jesus' body with spices and fragrances for His entombment. It was said that the water on it could heal, so I dipped a cloth which happened to be in my pocket into it. Amazing!

There was so much to see at the tomb or Edicule and such a long line of people waiting in line that finally the guide said he would show us something else in another place. With that, we left the church building and moved on to another site called the Garden Tomb. During this time, the guide disappeared for a time. Meanwhile, we had communion in the garden and visited a "hewn out of rock" tomb that says, "He is not here. He is Risen." He has indeed! Praise God!

Still feeling like I was in severe shock but altogether fine, I sat in the garden and listened to the birds singing and took photos all around me. It was very peaceful. All at once, the guide was there behind me coming from a souvenir shop.

"Come," he said. "Follow me, the photos are here."

An Arab guy with our group was standing by the wall outside the shop with an armload of photos.

"How much?" I asked him and took two, one for my sister and one for myself.

Going back into the souvenir shop, I handed her one and then turned back outside where the line to the photos was now long. I followed the ones who had their purchases to a cool shade on the street to wait for the others and the guide to tell us where we were to go next. After their purchases were made, the guide led us to where the bus was waiting to take us to the hotel.

CHAPTER 7

He is Everywhere!

It is a good thing to give thanks unto the LORD, and to sing praises unto thy name, O most High: To shew forth thy lovingkindness in the morning, and thy faithfulness every night, Upon an instrument of ten strings, and upon the psaltery; upon the harp with a solemn sound. For thou, LORD, hast made me glad through thy work: I will triumph in the works of thy hands. O LORD, how great are thy works! and thy thoughts are very deep.
(Psalm 92:1-5)

Excited to find out what this day had in store for us, the tour group boarded the bus for a short ride to the great walls surrounding Jerusalem. After walking a short distance to what is called The Hidden Gate, the Israeli antiquities director pointed out what is assumed to be the place of the judgment seat where Jesus stood, bound before Pilate and the crowd.

A placard for the gate says, "The Ottoman city wall is sealed but steps adjacent to it reveal a secret. They allude to the existence of a gate or postern in the city wall from the time of the Second Temple. Presumably this gate led to Herod's palace which was located nearby."

The group moved on to the Zion Gate. There the director points out the bullet holes in the walls and we can see that the Zion Gate is riddled with holes large enough to see the sky through. He explains how a balcony type of feature on the wall over the arch was used to drop stones or pour hot water or oil down on anyone trying to break in at the gate in ancient times as a type of defense mechanism.

The tour group leaves the walls behind to go to Mount Zion outside the walls on the buses. A beautiful blue-and-white church turns out to be the destination and the guide informs us that this is St. Peter's Church of Galicantu which was built and is maintained by the Catholics. On the inside are paintings of Peter with the cock crowing and a four-foot-hole with a railing around it where one can look down into the hill to see the ancient caves where the church was possibly located in Peter's time. Moving slowly down narrow steps to the bottom of the cave to a small room that is crowded, we turn around to go single file back to the top and outside again. The hill is covered with ancient steps and stones and caves.

Boarding the buses again, we head toward Bethlehem of Judea, now called Bethlehem of Palestine, on modern highways in heavy traffic. There are hotels and mansions built beside Bedouin huts and sheep farms. The media always shows the huts and sheep farms and unless one visits here, they will never know that just beside the huts are mansions built by Palestinians who live and work in the USA and use these mansions for vacations. The Bedouins have always farmed this land and would not trade their way of life for anything. This is not a criticism of them, for it is what they know and what they want to do. Changing their way of life would be a struggle since it is like the old saying, "You can take the man out of the country, but you can't take the country out of the man." Farm life is a special life to have and live.

Bethlehem means *house of bread* and it is one of the oldest towns in Judea. Its earliest name was Ephrath or Ephratah and it is mentioned in Genesis 35:16-19 where it says,

> And they journeyed from Bethel; and there was but a little way to come to Ephrath: and Rachel travailed, and she had hard labour. And it came to pass, when she was in hard labor, that the midwife said unto her, Fear not; thou shalt have this son also. And it came to pass, as her soul was in departing, (for she died) that she called his name Benoni: but his father called him Benjamin. And Rachel died, and was buried in the way to Ephrath, which is Bethlehem.

Again, it is mentioned in many chapters of the Bible, and the Book of Ruth is a domestic history of Bethlehem. In Ruth 1:1-2 it is called Bethlehemjudah, but in Ruth 1:19 it states, "So they two went until they came to Bethlehem. And it came to pass, when they were come to Bethlehem, that all the city was moved about them, and they said, *Is* this Naomi?"

Bethlehem was the home of David in 1 Samuel 17:12. "Now David was the son of that Ephrathite of Bethlehemjudah, whose name *was* Jesse; and he had eight sons: and the man went among men *for* an old man in the days of Saul."

It was in Bethlehem that Jesus Christ was born as stated in Matthew 2:1-2.

> Now when Jesus was born in Bethlehem of Judaea in the days of Herod the king, behold, there came wise men from the east to Jerusalem, Saying, Where is he that is born King of the Jews? for we have seen his star in the east, and are come to worship him.

The modern town of Beit-lahm is located about six miles east of the main road from Jerusalem to Hebron. In order to enter Palestine, one must first pass through a check point station. Then new buildings going up are noticeable, most are quite palatial having white columns and porches and balconies. A new hospital and office complex were almost complete when I was on this trip. Of course, the portion of the wall the media always shows is filled with graffiti of many curse words and words of hatred while maintaining slogans wanting freedom.

There were older portions of the town that appeared was fortified against vandalism. Some walls had graffiti on them and most street signs were in Arabic and English, but not in Hebrew. Huge plastic crates outside shop doors held watermelons, boxes held lemons, and bananas hung in bunches from the porch rafters. Some shops looked really old while others appeared to be brand new. One old one was Ramzi Burgers and stated it sold hamburgers and fried chicken. It had a Christmas tree, ice cream cone, and a chicken in neon lights on the roof. A newer shop had Christmas lights across the doorway and announced Palace Sweets, Samsung, Canavati and AVA Brother's shops. Christmas lights were visible in the mall where we ate lunch in an open-air porch. We had chicken or falafel that was delicious and cold water to drink, although you could order stronger drinks if you wanted one. Thank you, Lord! Praise Your Holy Name!

After lunch, our Jewish guide was changed to a Christian guide from Bethlehem. This guide, a handsome fellow, took us on a walking tour from the mall that advertised Kentucky Fried Chicken and Coca-Cola on huge billboards on the side, up the streets to the Church of the Nativity. The oldest Christian church in existence was built by Empress Helena in AD 330. It is built over the grotto or cave where the Virgin Mary gave birth to Jesus Christ.

> And Joseph also went up from Galilee, out of the city of Nazareth, into Judaea, unto the city of David, which is called Bethlehem; (because he was of the house and lineage of David:) To be taxed with Mary his espoused wife, being great with child. And so it was, that, while they were there, the days were accomplished that she should be delivered. And she brought forth her firstborn son, and wrapped him in swaddling clothes, and laid him in a

> manger; because there was no room for them in the inn.
>
> Luke 2:4-7

Although the church is under reconstruction with scaffolding and beams visible everywhere, it did not detract from the holy presence there. The fourteen-point silver star beneath the altar in the grotto marks the traditional spot believed to be the place where the manger was placed and the birthplace of the Jesus Christ to the Virgin Mary.

Icons were everywhere! There were bright chandeliers, paintings, metallic impressions, all different artists' conceptualizations of the Virgin Mary and the baby Jesus. The cave went deeper and a smaller cave is said to have held twenty-four skeletons of babies found in the cave and are thought to be a group of babies killed under the edict given by King Herod when Jesus was born. And Matthew 2:16 states,

> Then Herod, when he saw that he was mocked of the wise men, was exceeding wroth, and sent forth, and slew all the children that were in Bethlehem, and in all the coasts thereof, from two years old and under, according to the time which he had diligently enquired of the wise men.

The cavern went deeper into more cave rooms and one held a rock hewn table-like structure that said it was the resting place where Elisha's body lay after his death. Moving on to the next room, it was darker with no icons or decor, just a plain cave and the end of the rooms. Turning toward the wall by the doorway to leave the cave, an apparition appeared to be watching but then disappeared when I tried to take a photo of it.

Unafraid but alone in the last cave, I made my way back to the tour group that had stopped beside the Elisha structure and then passed on to the outside to give others a chance to move through the cavern. Some of the group was gathering in the massive reconstruction of the church taking photos of the tiles under the sub-floor of a previous construction and then queuing to go to the Church of Saint Catherine.

The Church of Saint Catherine is a Catholic church or Franciscan monastery, next door to the Church of the Nativity. It is a large white church with golden arches above and icons or paintings on every wall under archways, shiny wooden pews, and a dark wood confessional in an alcove at the entrance. The guide showed us the bas-relief of the Tree of Jesse, a brass sculpture donated to the church by Pope Benedict XVI during his visit to the church in 2009. The sculpture depicts the olive tree as the Tree of Jesse that displays the linage of Jesus Christ from Abraham through Joseph and has a crowned figure designed as Jesus Christ at the top with open arms representing a blessing for all the earth. Opposite to it, in another alcove, was a colorful reproduction of Saint George and the Dragon.

The streets were hot and filled with sellers of everything imaginable as we made our way back to the mall to the buses. Signs advertised products from King, Samsung, Electrolux, LG, Phillips and many others in English and Arabic languages. A man was unloading a new LG washer and electric fans as the bus passed by his appliance store from a truck filled with boxes of every size. "O Little Town of Bethlehem" is no more; instead it stretches from all over the West Bank with modern buildings that are constructed from one neighborhood to the next, on hills, in valleys from interstate road to interstate road. To Christians who read the Holy Bible, this town will always be Bethlehem of Judea no matter what political-religious faction tries to take it from Israel, and it will always remain the birthplace of Jesus Christ, our Lord and Savior. Hallelujah!

CHAPTER 8

His Presence

> Be it known unto the king, that we went into the province of Judea, to the house of the great God, which is builded with great stones, and timber is laid in the walls, and this work goes fast on, and prospers in their hands.
> (Ezra 5:8)

The majesty of the Judean Wilderness and desert is something spectacular to see. The bright blue sky overhead contrasted with the tan, barren hills surrounding the highway on both sides. This is the place that is thought to be the place where David wrote the Book of Psalms. A sign indicated that sea level was 500 meters up the hillside. Sparse brown grass could be spotted in crevices in the landscape and scattered sheep and goat herders in remote hollows. This is a place that waits for the rainy season that meanwhile is supplemented by tanks of water to keep the animals and people thriving. These barren mountains have a presence about them like no other on earth.

An oasis here and there broke the monotony of the bareness of the Judean wilderness. Agriculture is evidenced in many places with patches of date palms. An oasis with a church with gold-domed spinnerets and crosses on top flying a Christian red cross came into view. A stone wall surrounded it. It was secluded with palm trees. Signs pointing to the "Kasser-Al-Yehud Baptism Site" came into view. Here there were fields planted with palm trees so far as the eye can see on the horizon on the Israel side. Signs announced that this is the Jordan-Israel border and wire fences separated the two countries land. Nearby is another large monastery behind walls of sand-colored stone blocks that blended with the desert sand. Kasser-Al-Yehud is believed to be the place where John was baptizing when Jesus came to him. The Gospel of John says that John the Baptist baptized in a region of Bethabara beyond the Jordan and he was challenged by the Pharisees there.

Some of the tour members bought baptismal gowns to be baptized. Although there was only one minister on our bus on the tour, he agreed to baptize those who wanted to be baptized. There was a platform and steps that led down into the river. River cane grew in brambles on both sides of the river and a monastery was across the river. Several tour groups were there and some were across the Jordan by the monastery. Some people wanted to wade into the water while others just dipped their toes into the water.

It was like a celebration with people taking photos and laughing and talking to each other. Doves flew across the river to the belfry of the monastery as a sign it was all right. The guide brought a fellow with a camera to take a group photo of the group by the Jordan. Then it was time to continue the journey into the Judean Wilderness. Fields of date palms in every stage of growth were being maintained on both sides of the road. Heavy machinery was gathering the old branches cast off by the trees making clean, stately rows.

Caves appear in the desert wilderness. It is no wonder that David hid here in caves in a place called Engedi.

In 1 Samuel 23:29 it states, "And David went up from there, and dwelt in strong holds at Engedi." And it continues in 1 Samuel 24:1-3

> And it came to pass, when Saul was returned from following the Philistines, that it was told him, saying, 'Behold, David is in the wilderness of Engedi.' Then Saul took three thousand chosen men out of all Israel, and went to seek David and his men upon the rocks of the wild goats. And he came to the sheepcotes by the way, where was a cave; and Saul went in to cover his feet: and David and his men remained in the sides of the cave.

On one side of the highway is the desert wilderness and on the other is the Dead Sea. Nubian Ibex or wild goats from David's time are spotted on the barren hillside coming down from the heights above. The herd seems to follow a line to the bottom of the hill and as the bus is stopped for road work, the guide points out that this is near Wadi David, an oasis watering hole in the desert.

Traveling on beside the Dead Sea, the shape of the mountain changed to become Masada. Masada means stronghold and is famous for the period of the Great Revolt of AD 66-74 in history. The souvenir and gift shop located at the foot of the mountain contained artifacts of pottery found on Masada. There are jars, bowls, water jugs, cooking pots, cups and other stone vessels in display cases. Eager to see the rest of the site, the group boarded a cable car to ride to the top of the mountain, taking photos along the way. Although a path called The Snake Path leads to the mountain top, the cable car came to a jolting halt inside a platform where everyone could dismount and follow the path to the entrance in the mountain.

The guide led the way up paths and steps to the side of the mountain where the Dead Sea was almost in view in its entirety. There was a spectacular view of the surrounding Negev desert from the top of Masada. Many of the buildings were under reconstruction and had the original stones in place to show where buildings stood. Tiles and plaster were in view to show how richly decorated the insides of these buildings were in the days of Herod. The guide showed a model of Masada and how Herod's palace was perched on the frontal edge with swimming pool and splendid rooms. Mosaic floors with Jewish motifs popular in Jewish art of the Herodian period were in evidence along with a synagogue with stone benches. Several hundred inscribed shards of pottery were found including some with the names of Yigael Yadin and Ben Ya'it and are thought to be the lots drawn in Josephus Flavius' story on the last night of the revolt.

The water cistern held two women with children who lived after the mayhem of the Roman attack on Masada. The guide demonstrated using a model of Masada of how water was collected through the use of two aqueducts. The rainy season fed the rain into many cisterns on the mountain. He then guided everyone to see the actual cisterns quarried by Herod to fill his pools and baths.

Artifacts including silver shekel coins, sheets of papyrus, fragments of scrolls, glass vessels, and bone implements as well as the pay record of a Roman cavalryman in the Tenth Legion were found in a corner of a room. Moving on to the breaching point to look at the place where the Romans finally out-maneuvered the Jewish patriots, it seems impossible that anyone could have come up the side of that mountain even with the Roman ingenuity of building. Unused stones used for defense still lay in piles like cannon balls. Although it is a bright sunny day, sadness creeps in at the enormity of what happened here. The heat finally gets to some in the tour group, so it is time to go back to the cable car and down the mountain.

Stuck in traffic on the Dead Sea highway, there were fantastic views on the way to Qumran where the Dead Sea Scrolls were found. Upon reaching Qumran, lunch is served in a restaurant in the souvenir shop building.

The air was so thick with God's presence that I just wanted to sit and soak in it. Then a movie was shown in a theater on the history of how the Dead Sea Scrolls were found. Filing through the museum, the Scriptorium includes a desk, seat, ink wells and scrolls found by archaeologists. The main scrolls were found by shepherds in caves in the mountain. The guide took us on a tour of Qumran and gave the history as he points out the special features of the site.

In the Scriptorium, the scrolls that were copied date from the late Hellenistic to the early Roman period. Not mentioned in the Bible, the writings show the religious traditions of the people of that period through the ritual baths or mitzvah of the

Jewish people. There were rooms where artifacts were found that had signs describing the artifacts and their usage. There were also rooms designed to look like the living quarters, or the scriptorium where rows of scribes copied the scrolls. This is an amazing place in sight of the Dead Sea.

In the Dead Sea, the saline content is so high, you can float on the water. Many people were there grabbing handfuls of slimy green sea mud and covering their bodies in it. Monsters coming up from the deep, they emerge as new creatures with soft skin and hair. A Chinese group was there slathering the green stuff over themselves and each other and having a wonderful time playing like children in a mud puddle. My sister was first to join them in the sea. Some people believe there is healing in the waters. For me, trying to float was an ordeal. Laying back and sinking like a rock at first, my feet floated to the top and I could not stand back up. Two ladies standing nearby each got an arm and pulled me upright again and rescued me. The water went into my mouth and eyes, causing my eyes to sting. One of the ladies had a bottle of water which she offered to pour in my mouth and over my eyes. How soothing that was and my skin was incredibly soft for days! That mud is wonderful stuff.

CHAPTER 9

Seeing Him

Then Samuel took the horn of oil, and anointed him in the midst of his brethren: and the Spirit of the LORD came upon David from that day forward. So Samuel rose up, and went to Ramah.
(1 Samuel 16:13)

The conclusion of the tour in 2015 included taking a scenic route through the countryside passing cities, towns, and villages in search of the boy king, David. Bridge building and road construction were in view as well as farms and fields of fruit trees. An ancient site in the middle of farm and cities held historical buildings and a huge round disk that appeared to be made of concrete and stones thought to go along with some type of sun god worship with other ancient parts of buildings showing through the grass.

The scripture read by the guide was 1 Samuel 5. Although this site was on a small hill, it was in the Valley of Elah. Here the Philistines would get on one side of the mountain and yell at the people of Israel on the other side of the mountain. The scripture read for this is the story of David and Goliath.

And Saul and the men of Israel were gathered together, and pitched by the valley of Elah, and set the battle in array against the Philistines. And the Philistines stood on a mountain on the one side, and Israel stood on a mountain on the other side: and there was a valley between them. And there went out a champion out of the camp of the Philistines, named Goliath, of Gath, whose height was six cubits and a span. And he had an helmet of brass upon his head, and he was armed with a coat of mail; and the weight of the coat was five thousand shekels of brass. And he had greaves of brass upon his legs, and a target of brass between his shoulders. And the staff of his spear was like a weaver's beam; and his spear's head weighed six hundred shekels of iron: and one bearing a shield went before him. And he stood and cried unto the armies of Israel, and said unto them, Why are you come out to set your battle in array? Am not I a Philistine, and you servants to Saul? Choose you a man for you, and let him come down to me. If he is able to fight with me, and to kill me, then will we be your servants: but if I prevail against him, and kill him, then shall you will be our servants, and serve us. And the Philistine said, I defy the armies of Israel this day; give me a man, that we may fight together. When Saul and all Israel heard those words of the Philistine, they were dismayed, and greatly afraid.

1 Samuel 17:2-11

However, we all know there was one Israelite that was not afraid and that was David, the anointed. More scriptures were read as we observed that we were in this valley with mountains on all sides, just as they were in David's day.

Passing farm land and some ancient ruins, the guide informed us that this was the place where Moloch was worshiped. On the brink of the hill was an ancient stone fire pit where the Ammonites sacrificed children by throwing them into a fire. Moloch was the national god of fire and was a consuming, destroying, and purifying fire, or so they thought. It is mentioned in Amos 5:26 and in 1 Kings 11:7, Solomon built a high place for it on the Mount of Olives and until the days of Josiah, this worship continued. This god became Chemosh to the Moabites. However; in 2 Kings 23, something happened.

> And he [Josiah] defiled Topheth, which is in the valley of the children of Hinnom, that no man might make his son or his daughter to pass through the fire to Molech. And he took away the horses that the kings of Judah had given to the sun, at the entering in of the house of the LORD, by the chamber of Nathanmelech the chamberlain, which was in the suburbs, and burned the chariots of the sun with fire."
>
> 2 Kings 23:10-11

Next stop is a goat and sheep pasture where it is believed that David met Goliath in 1 Samuel 17:34-47. As the guide read these scriptures, a honey buzzard circled overhead and the sun beamed down on the pasture. The goat sheep herd kicked up dust as they milled around.

The tour bus traces the route that David might have taken the head of Goliath back to Jerusalem. Some believe the head was buried on the Hill of Golgatha where Jesus Christ was crucified thus the name Golgatha. On Road 1 back to Jerusalem, there are conifer forests and spacious views of the surrounding country. New buildings are going up, new vineyards are being planted and finally the Holy City, Jerusalem. At Zion Gate, the group gathers to see Hezekiah's Wall or the Broad Wall. A sign states that it was built over 2,600 years ago as part of the wall surrounding Jerusalem's western hill during the reign of King Hezekiah about the eighth century BC. The seven-meter-wide wall that was excavated for a length of sixty-five meters by archeologists is seen underneath the modern streets and may be what Isaiah refers to in Isaiah 22:10-11:

> And ye have numbered the houses of Jerusalem, and the houses have ye broken down to fortify the wall. Ye made also a ditch between the two walls for the water of the old pool: but ye have not looked unto the maker thereof, neither had respect unto him that fashioned it long ago.

In the afternoon, the group is led down the street to some stairs and beside the stairs is a circular display case with a golden menorah enclosed. Passing many people on the stairs handing out red string, playing guitars, or just sitting in the shade, the group advances on the Western Wailing Wall. This is the largest open-air synagogue in the world and the only place that Jews and Christians are allowed to pray near the Temple Mount. It was amazing to see the numbers of people visiting that day. The guide explained that the women were allowed on one side and the men were allowed on the other side of a partition separating the space in front of the Wall. My sister carried a plastic bag with slips of paper with prayers from people at her church to place in the wall.

The night before, thinking that I would pray to the Lord without slips of paper, the Lord distinctly asked if I remembered the song I had brought with me. I replied "yes" and He said to fold the song and place it into the wall. The amazing thing is that no one knew that I had the song in my luggage. I didn't tell anyone and I didn't show anyone. A few weeks before the trip, I felt I needed to find and print the song and I thought it was all me because I am not a singer. That is how I know this was a supernatural voice of God thing. I had the song folded in my pocket.

Police and IDF marched across the open area to the police station. People milled around the space from everywhere. I wondered who would lead the women down to the wall since the guide was lining up the men to follow him to the men's side of the area. He was telling the men their heads had to be covered with a cap they could pick up in the men's area and ladies could pick up a scarf if they wished in the ladies' area of the synagogue. He folded his tour cap and put it in his back pocket. I don't know why, but a thought ran through my mind that if he put on the little cap or kippah, I might faint. Then he looked around at me with the briefest of glances from those beautiful brown eyes, and all of a sudden, a vision of him holding me flashes through my mind, and I am satiated with love and clinging to him.

My arm winds around his neck and my hand threads his soft black hair through my fingers behind his head as he holds me close. Then like a flash of light, this tiny vision was gone. So as soon as the women walked down to the wall, I took out the folded song and crammed it into one of the cracks between two of the huge blocks in the wall and then turned and moved away so someone else could reach the wall. My sister deposited her prayer slips in the wall then stayed beside the wall to pray.

I told the Lord what I had to say and then I sang the song as I walked all around the area, taking photos of people. And that song is from verses in Mark 11:9 "And they that went before, and they that followed, cried, saying, Hosanna; Blessed is he that cometh in the name of the Lord:" and in Matthew 23:39, "For I say unto you, Ye shall not see me henceforth, till ye shall say, Blessed is he that comes in the name of the Lord." Hosanna! I looked through the lattice to the men's side and saw Him. Oh, my God, Lord Jesus, Holy Spirit, how I love you!

Meeting again, the bus took us to the hotel to shower and dress for dinner before going to the airport in Tel Aviv to catch a flight to the USA. After packing and taking our suitcases down to the bus, the guide was loading our bus when they told him that he was on the other bus. My sister poked me and said to ask the guide if we were on the right bus which I did. He said yes, that he would see me at dinner. The thought ran unexpectedly through my mind, *not if I see you first.*

An astonishing thing happened at dinner! Our group was eating, chatting, making jokes, and laughing. I laughed a little too loudly I thought and I turned to the table behind us to apologize for my rudeness and it looked like golden beams of light was coming from the guide's eyes. Even though he looked quickly down at his plate, I was pretty sure I saw it, although in the next nanosecond my mind went blank and I forgot it. My sister, who kept peeking around me, wanted to leave the table.

Suddenly, His voice in my head said, "Do not be like that other woman. Just get up and walk away without looking back." The memory of Lot's wife flashed through my mind as that other woman. It was the hardest thing I have ever done, but I want to do what Jesus says regardless of what anyone wants. I could not look back so I suggested that we would meet the others in the foyer or on the balcony for one last look at Jerusalem from the hotel before leaving for the airport. Then I got up and walked out the door.

After meeting again in the airport, I could not even say goodbye. My mind kept saying this is not goodbye; it is until I return again. I passed through Tel Aviv like a scatterbrain because I lost my ability to hear and I had to keep asking my sister where to go and what to do. The security person kept repeating his instructions and finally resorted to hand signals.

Then after sleeping and reaching Philly airport, I forgot to remove my money pouch strapped around my waist and it had slipped up around my back. I was strip-searched in a tiny room by two women who even looked through and counted my money. I didn't know if He would be invisible or not on the x-ray machine. At times I would remember Him but most of the time, I did not remember anything and I did not question why I would think about any of this since I had no memory of it. Thankfully I was allowed to rejoin my sister and board the plane and then to fly on home without incident. Praise His name forever! However; this story did not end here.

CHAPTER 10

Memories Return

"The LORD hath appeared of old unto me, saying,
Yea, I have loved thee with an everlasting love:
therefore with lovingkindness have I drawn thee."
(Jeremiah 31:3)

My memory began to return about three weeks after the tour. I wrestled with not knowing what happened and prayed for the Lord to reveal it to me. He did not let it come back all at once but started showing me verses to read in the Bible. He started with Jeremiah 3:14 which says, "Turn, O backsliding children, saith the LORD; for *I am married unto you*: and I will take you one of a city, and two of a family, and I will bring you to Zion:" It was I am married to you that stuck out in this verse. I was astounded because I never noticed this verse before. I think I would have remembered it. Talk about shock and awe! That is how I felt. This warm love poured over my head and tingled down to my toes. I was giddy and lightheaded. The enormity of what I had read just blew my mind.

He showed me this verse in Isaiah 54:5-11 that states,

> For thy Maker is thine husband; the LORD of hosts is his name; and thy Redeemer the Holy One of Israel; The God of the whole earth shall he be called. For the LORD hath called thee as a woman forsaken and grieved in spirit, and a wife of youth, when thou wast refused, saith thy God. For a small moment have I forsaken thee; but with great mercies will I gather thee. In a little wrath I hid my face from thee for a moment; but with everlasting kindness will I have mercy on thee, saith the LORD thy Redeemer. For this is as the waters of Noah unto me: for as I have sworn that the waters of Noah should no more go over the earth; so have I sworn that I would not be wroth with thee, nor rebuke you. For the mountains shall depart, and the hills be removed; but my kindness shall not depart from thee, neither shall the covenant of my peace be removed, saith the LORD that hath mercy on you.

This verse caused me to have a humbling, tender worshipping moment when I cried for happiness and sadness at the same time. He knows my story. He is so awesome!

On June 22, 2015, God gave me these scriptures. What is the meaning of the mystery revealed in Romans 11:25-29? This is from the New Testament or *Brit Chadashah* in Hebrew.

> For I would not, brethren, that ye should be ignorant of this mystery, lest ye should be wise in your own conceits; that blindness in part is happened to Israel, until the fullness of the Gentiles be come in. And so all Israel shall

be saved: as it is written, There shall come out of Sion the Deliverer, and shall turn away ungodliness from Jacob: For this is my covenant unto them, when I shall take away their sins. As concerning the gospel, they are enemies for your sakes: but as touching the election, they are beloved for the fathers' sakes. For the gifts and calling of God are without repentance.

Romans 11:25-29

He showed me this in Hebrews 8:8-13:

For finding fault with them, he saith, Behold, the days come, saith the Lord, when I will make a new covenant with the house of Israel and with the house of Judah: Not according to the covenant that I made with their fathers in the day when I took them by the hand to lead them out of the land of Egypt; because they continued not in my covenant, and I regarded them not, saith the Lord. For this is the covenant that I will make with the house of Israel after those days, saith the Lord; I will put my laws into their mind, and write them in their hearts: and I will be to them a God, and they shall be to me a people: And they shall not teach every man his neighbor, and every man his brother, saying, Know the Lord: for all shall know me, from the least to the greatest. For I will be merciful to their unrighteousness, and their sins and their iniquities will I remember no more. In that he saith, A new covenant, he hath made the first old. Now that which decays and waxes old is ready to vanish away."

And in Matthew 24:30-31 He tells me about His return, "And then shall appear the sign of the Son of man in heaven: and then shall all the tribes of the earth mourn, and they shall see the Son of man coming in the clouds of heaven with power and great glory."

Then this was pointed out to me.

> There is neither Jew nor Greek, there is neither bond nor free, there is neither male nor female: for ye are all one in Christ Jesus. And if ye be Christ's, then are ye Abraham's seed, and heirs according to the promise.
>
> Galatians 3:28-29

Isaiah 13:12 states, "I will make a man more precious than fine gold; even a man than the golden wedge of Ophir."

A question that keeps coming to my mind is Jesus Christ already here on the planet Earth with us again? It is strange how you can read a verse and it not make any sense and then you read it another time and it makes amazing sense. The grace of God is so rich and so pure.

I was creating a presentation for a Bible college class with my photos from the tour and I reflected on my attitude. Going up the stairs to The Place of the Skull, Calvary or Golgotha, my backpack had felt like it weighed a ton and the sun was so hot it seemed unbearable. I had no idea where we were going, just that the guide had said it was the Church of the Holy Sepulcher and there was a ladder on the roof that was called the Immovable Ladder. Even though I had read about all this in my literature for the trip, it now seems odd that I could not remember anything about what I had read. Nothing!

There was no thought that Jesus Christ had climbed this steep hill suffering from being beaten, sweating from the intense heat and with a heavy wooden cross on His back or for what He had suffered when He got there. My own physical limitations were all that seemed important and my one selfish desire seemed to be to just follow the lady in front of me and get up those steep stairs. I am embarrassed to think that a little physical discomfort made me unaware of the most important place on earth but I guess that was the setup for what was to happen. This was the place where Jesus' stripes healed me and His blood saved me and the world from our sins. No other place on earth is as important as this rock. None! It is the place where He gave His life as a willing sacrifice for me. He now exists as the mediator between all men and God to hear and to bear our petitions to Him. There is no greater love than that. He is love!

Strange little things started happening to me. I went to a short revival at a church and I was talking to the Lord in my mind and I said that I should have told everyone goodbye at the airport and at least gave them a hug. This young man stands up in the front of the church, leaves his wife and children, passes ten pews and stops in front of me and asks if he can give me a hug. I said yes, but I was truly surprised. He gave me a gentle hug and then went on down the aisle. Still another strange incident happened when I stepped out onto the porch to see why it was getting so dark outside. A couple of dark storm clouds were filling the sky. I looked above me at the small patch of blue sky between the two cloud masses. A pair of cloud glasses formed above me with blue sky for the lenses. Then as I thanked God and Jesus for them, each of the lenses turned into a perfect heart one at a time. Truly amazing!

He gave me Ezekiel 16:8-14 that read,

> Now when I passed by thee, and looked upon thee, behold, thy time was the time of love; and I spread my skirt over you, and covered thy nakedness: yea, I sware unto thee, and entered into a covenant with you, saith the Lord GOD, and thou became mine. Then washed I you with water; yea, I thoroughly washed away thy blood from you, and I anointed you with oil. I clothed you also with broidered work, and shod you with badgers' skin, and I girded you about with fine linen, and I covered you with silk. I decked you also with ornaments, and I put bracelets upon your hands, and a chain on your neck. And I put a jewel on your forehead, and earrings in your ears, and a beautiful crown upon your head. Thus you were decked with gold and silver; and your raiment was of fine linen, and silk, and broidered work; you did eat fine flour, and honey, and oil: and you were exceeding beautiful, and you did prosper into a kingdom. And your renown went forth among the heathen for your beauty: for it was perfect through my comeliness, which I had put upon you, said the Lord GOD.

What a love song from God that is. Some think it may have been meant about Jerusalem, but God uses scripture to talk to individuals too.

Jesus Christ says in John 14:16-20,

> And I will pray the Father, and he shall give you another Comforter, that he may abide with you for ever; Even the Spirit of truth; whom the world cannot receive, because it seeth him not, neither knoweth him: but you know him; for he dwells with you, and shall be in you. I will not leave you comfortless: *I will come to you.* Yet a little while, and the world sees me no more; but you see me: because I live, you shall live also. At that day you shall know that *I am in my Father, and you in me, and I in you.*

The Holy Spirit or Holy Ghost is the third person in the Trinity. The Holy Spirit is the one who comforts us, guides us, teaches us, shares truth with us, and empowers us to live daily with God. Through Him, the quickening that shows love, favor, wisdom, miracles, signs, and so much more shows up. What an awesome being He is! I have a very close connection with Him night and day. He fills my every need in every way!

He is my constant companion and is everything to me. He is my cloud by day and my pillar of fire by night!

CHAPTER 11

2016 Holy Spirit in Me

"At that day ye shall know that I am in my Father,
and ye in me, and I in you."
(John 14:20)

Almost a year later in 2016, the Holy Spirit impressed on me to go back to Israel. He continued this for several months. Finally, I started looking to see if there are any tours going at such a time as this. One tour as all that was left in late May 2016. The tour was only two weeks away. I thought at this late date, it was impossible to get the money to go and to get the tour to let us go, or to get anyone to go with me. Then *out of the blue*, my sister said she will go with me. I was surprised. I looked for the money and there it was where I never noticed before. Amazing. I called the tour host and they say no, it is too late to join them. There was just no way to get flights set up.

A week later, I get a phone call from the tour folks that we can go, but they need the money right away, plus other steps need to be followed and it must be all done in one day. I could not believe how everything fell into place and instead of graduating from a specific Bible College which I had planned to do, my sister and I were flying out of Atlanta on our way to Israel.

> Likewise, the Spirit also helps our infirmities: for we know not what we should pray for as we ought: but the Spirit itself makes intercession for us with groanings which cannot be uttered.
>
> Romans 8:26

The plane arrived in a drenching downpour of snow and rain. A shuttle bus took us to the airport, from our hotel and let us off. That was at 8:30 a.m. From that time until 12:30 p.m., my sister and I lugged our suitcases through the airport. One person sent us to Gate 1 by train, then another back to Gate 2 by train, then another to Gate 39 by foot. These gates were far apart, and we ran the entire way not knowing when our flight would leave since no one could tell us where it was located. After twelve hours of sleeplessness, a numbing effect helped us to survive the wait. At long last, four hours later and after much frustration, a Gate 38 appeared with our flight. We joined Jews and Israelis on an Israeli airplane and were so thankful to board and get on our way. Although we did not know it, there were three of us going and we met the other lady when we got to our seats on the plane. We were supposed to meet the rest of the tour at 4:30 p.m. that day in Tel Aviv.

That didn't happen. Arriving too late to catch the tour group, we were met by the tour host who ordered a taxi for us but it took another three hours for it to arrive from Galilee and so it was 10:30 p.m. before we arrived at the hotel in Galilee. By this time, I was exhausted. Our tour guide had waited up for us and stepped out of the shadows and asked for me. I immediately shied away from him, although he seemed nice and had stayed up to tell us the itinerary for the next day and that he had ordered food delivered to our rooms so we could have something for dinner.

Crossing the Galilee, the next day, we met our tour group and tour leader. This trip on the Galilee was different from the first one. Only the American flag was raised and the U.S. national anthem sung. The two guides each took turns pointing out some specific landmarks around the sea. The pastor read the scriptures and some merchants sold souvenirs. Our group of three went in together and purchased Galilee stone necklaces for each of us. Arriving on the other side of the sea, we walked through the museum but didn't stop. We went on to the buses and to the Mount of Beatitudes Church where the guides arranged a place for the pastor to read scriptures and talk.

The message was *be blessed* because everyone fits into one of these Beatitudes; to be comforted, to inherit, to be filled, to have mercy, to see God, to be called Sons of God and to see the kingdom of heaven. Everyone should, "Rejoice, and be exceeding glad: for great is your reward in heaven: for so persecuted they the prophets which were before you" (Matthew 5:12).

Jesus preached here to thousands sitting down without the benefit of loud microphones, headsets, or volume speakers.

When you are lacking in the Spirit, you are guaranteed to get into the kingdom because the kingdom belongs to the unworthy. Read the Bible and when you hunger for God, you will be filled. Those that mourn will be comforted, the meek will find strength, those who hunger and thirst for righteousness will be filled, the merciful will find mercy by giving to others, the pure of heart will see God by glorifying Jesus not themselves, the peacemakers will calm troubled waters not stir them up even though you can't be at peace with everyone. An enemy is someone who persecutes you just because they want to pursue you to the very end. Usually you are convicting them, even though this is someone who doesn't like you just because they want to. Regardless of who we are, we are blessed! Beatitudes lead to great attitudes!

We were blessed to go on to Capernaum to see where Peter's mother-in-law lived and the canopy building above the house foundation provided a clear view of the structure. The observatory allowed one to take a photo centered on this house. From its windows a clear view of the surrounding Galilee and the ancient ruins of the Roman era synagogue beside her house. The guide held up visual aids to show the foundation and how the house may have looked during Jesus' visit to Peter's mother-in-law.

And again, he entered into Capernaum after some days; and it was noised that he was in the house. And straightway many were gathered together, insomuch that there was no room to receive them, no, not so much as about the door: and he preached the word unto them. And they come unto him, bringing one sick of the palsy, which was borne of four. And when they could not come nigh unto him for the press, they uncovered the roof where he was: and when they had broken it up, they let down the bed wherein the sick of the palsy lay. When Jesus saw their faith, he said unto the sick of the palsy, Son, thy sins be forgiven thee."

Mark 2:1-12

The church's number one job is to break down barriers and reach people. It takes a team effort to do it. What excites God? God is excited by friends that share. Trust God to meet your needs for He is in the house! Invite friends and share with each other. This man could not have met Jesus and been healed if his friends had not cared enough to help him. Imagine dragging him up on the roof, taking the roof apart and lowering him down into the crowd in front of Jesus. What faith they had that Jesus could help their friend and it was *their faith* not his that Jesus saw and he healed him. Not only was he healed but his sins were forgiven, and the greatest miracle is that he was saved. God's son had to die in order for people to be saved! Go, share the gospel and spread the word that these same miracles take place today.

Moving on to Caesarea Philippi, scriptures are read first in the cool shade near the rushing waters of Hermon Springs from Mark 8:27 and Matthew 16:16. God will reveal Jesus to us and Jesus will build His church on that revelation. Commit to spreading the gospel and being involved with the church that Jesus built!

Leaving the cool shade, we walked on to the grotto where in centuries past, children and adults were drowned as sacrifices to try to obtain favor with gods. One sign said it was the temple of Pan and the dancing goats. Built in 220 BC, only parts of it survived, among them, the north wall, part of a semicircular hall, and a semicircular niche behind it. This same structure is depicted on the Panias city coin showing a niche with a statue in it. Pan appears in a niche playing a flute to three dancing goats in the hall. The musicians sat in the stairway adjacent to the niche while the goats danced. This ritual was supposed to ensure the fertility of the herds. Did this work? Probably not, but some people believed it did. Believe on Jesus Christ for He is the foundation and He does not fall like statues or marble columns and break into pieces! Commit to him alone. We moved through broken columns, pieces of fallen walls, and down the path back to the buses leaving this legacy of these gods.

The evening shade is coming over the sides of the mountain as we reach the Valley of the Doves. The group listens as the guide reads scriptures pertaining to doves. "O my dove, that art in the clefts of the rock, in the secret places of the stairs, let me see thy countenance, let me hear thy voice; for sweet is thy voice, and thy countenance is comely." (Song of Songs 2:14)

Doves were raised for sacrifices and food and the wild doves build their homes in the holes or cots of the mountain here. Doves and turtle doves were the only birds that could be offered in sacrifice according to Mosaic Law because they were considered clean fowl. The dove was a harbinger of peace for Noah who let one out of the ark (Gen 8:8, 10). It was the emblem of purity in Psalms 68:13, and it is the symbol of the Holy Spirit throughout the Bible. The mountains on both sides of the valley were pocked with holes for the doves to live in and the setting sun illuminates the mountains in rosy light. It was a peaceful place with cows drinking from the stream and a local woman with two teenagers checking a pipe to ensure water was flowing through it. They were living across the highway from the valley. Doves cooed loudly, sounding a chorus, as we filed back down the valley to the buses and thus ending the first day in Israel.

The next day's itinerary is given on the way to the hotel. Baptism at Yardenit is first so wear appropriate swimming clothing under the rented gowns.

CHAPTER 12

Baptism in the Jordan River

"Therefore, we are buried with him by baptism into death: that like as Christ was raised up from the dead by the glory of the Father, even so we also should walk in newness of life." (Romans 6:4)

Jordan River: Yardenit Baptismal Site

Wearing our swimming suits under our outer clothing enabled those wishing to be baptized again, as on outward gesture in the Jordan River like Jesus did. We quickly dressed in the white gowns belonging to the souvenir shop and lined up beside the river. The tour pastor first baptized his helper, and then together, they baptized each of us in turn. The river was more than waist deep, but there were metal railings to hang onto to keep from falling on slippery stones on the bottom or floating away in the current which was quite strong on this day.

I anxiously waded to the pastor and answered his questions. With a quick swish, I was laid back into the river water and brought up again. I thought it was over but the pastor said, "Let's do this one again. We didn't wet her hair enough."

I held my nose and *swoosh*, I was back under the water deep enough to see the bubbling green water above me. Upright again, I put my hands in the air and said a big hallelujah! Praise the Lord!

My sister was waiting and we went to the dressing rooms, showered, and put on clean clothes. After the cold river water, they felt really good. The entire baptismal service was videotaped and put on DVDs, so we purchased one from the cameraman to keep for a memory and souvenir.

The buses moved on to Nazareth and the Mount of Precipice with a view of the Jezreel Valley below. It was a patchwork in various shades of greens, browns and the blue of irrigation water ponds and the white of city buildings.

However; this time it was amazingly quiet around the city except for the calls of birds and voices of people. Boarding the buses to descend into the Jezreel Valley, one did not know where to look first. On each side of the highway, hay fields and fruit tree orchards stretched as far as the eye could see. What an beautiful place! The highway led us to the other side of the Jezreel Valley to Megiddo or Tel Megiddo. At Megiddo, the group listened to scriptures read by the pastor pertaining to the site, including 2 Chronicles 1:14 that says, "And Solomon gathered chariots and horsemen: and he had a thousand and four hundred chariots, and twelve thousand horsemen, which he placed in the chariot cities, and with the king at Jerusalem."

Many layers of building can be seen here on the Tel as well as a deep storage pit for grain for horses in Solomon's stables and a humungous cistern that goes deep under ground to water.

After this interesting site, the buses take the tour group into Lebanon to Liali al-Carmel Restaurant for authentic Druze food. The restaurant was bright and cheery even though much of the group ate *al fresco* on the porch and the delicious food was chicken or falafel with vegetables.

Traveling on to Mount Carmel for a 360-degree view of the Jezreel Valley from atop the Franciscan Monastery, we see Mount Tabor in the distance. The pastor read scriptures from 1 Kings 18:19-21 about the people's choice between God and Baal. The time passed pleasantly and the group loaded the buses for Caesarea Maritima.

Just as people did during the time of Herod, the group sat on the rows of seats from the top of the theater. Herod's throne was pointed out as his royal theater seat in the center of the rows.

Outside the theater, the guide pointed out pieces of Roman statues like heads, hands and feet. He said they were cut off by unknown persons probably during or after the war of AD 70. Other artifacts are scattered around along with tall columns of ancient buildings. We descend to the level of the hippodrome and the Mediterranean Sea to explore that area. It was while we were below the upper platform at sea level that a miraculous thing happened! I was walking up the beach toward the platform where the guide was standing. He stretched out his arms and stood like a cross. My sister beside me put her arms out and did the same thing back at him. He looked at me, dropped his arms, then put them out again and seemed to indicate that I should do the same, so I put my arms out and looked back at him.

My sister and I walked on toward the platform when suddenly in my right ear I hear the words, "I love you." I was astounded. I stopped. Then looked around to see who was speaking but no one was there. I could hear the guide talking to someone on the platform in my earpiece and when we got to the point where we could see on top of it, he was talking to one of the fellows on the tour. I made it to the bus and my seat before crying. I put my head to the window like I was looking at something and I sobbed. Those three little words just got to me. Thank God, only He heard my crying! Jesus is my Rock that I cling to.

CHAPTER 13

His Beginning

Away in a manger, no crib for a bed,
The little Lord Jesus laid down His sweet head;
The stars in the sky looked down where He lay,
The little Lord Jesus, asleep on the hay.

The cattle are lowing, the Baby awakes,
But little Lord Jesus no crying He makes,
I love Thee, Lord Jesus, look down from the sky,
And stay by my cradle till morning is nigh.

"Away in the Manger," author unknown.

The buses rolled on to Jerusalem and our hotels to stay in. Nice rooms and delicious supper and breakfast tend to refresh us all. The tour moves on to the "Shepherd's Fields" where we see archeological digs of ancient millstones and pottery. The group enjoys more scriptures about the shepherds who were awake that night of Christ's birth. The pastor asks, "Why were they awake? Their animals would be stolen or taken by animals. They were protecting their animals. Shepherds walked with a staff with a hook to pull the sheep back into the fold. Sheep that escaped had to have their legs broken but only perfect sheep could be sold and used for sacrifice under the law in Leviticus. The shepherd carries the lamb so that it will be pure and clean. Jesus was our perfect sacrifice and that is why His bones were not broken on the cross."

The Shepherd's Fields raised sacrificial lambs for all sacrifices. Bethlehem, Nazareth, Jerusalem; each city gives a picture of Jesus. Micah 5:2 "But thou, Bethlehem Ephratah, though thou be little among the thousands of Judah, yet out of thee shall he come forth unto me that is to be ruler in Israel; whose goings forth have been from of old, from everlasting." Bethlehem means house of bread or body; Ephratah means fruitful, wine, or blood." God keeps His promises! After the group choir sang "Oh, Beautiful Star of Bethlehem," we moved on to explore our surroundings by the Good Shepherd Fountain, the Grotto Cave where the shepherds lived and on to the Gloria in Excelsis Church run by the Franciscans. This church is said to be built on the site where the angels visited the shepherds in the field. Inside the church were murals depicting scenes from the night Christ was born, painted in glorious colors. What an awesome God we serve!

Back on the tour buses, we traveled a short distance to Bethlehem in Palestine, not Judea now, where we follow the guides to a building with a factory down under it that makes olive wood figurines. The proprietor shows how the factory workers use a machine to duplicate and carve the same figurines and how others use machines to make unique pieces that are large and in different shapes. He says that it is against the law to cut an olive tree down, but if a branch falls off, they can gather those and dry them to use for the figurines. The scent of the saw dust and the smell of the paint fumes are so strong that he hastens the group up the stairs to the shop. The details on the pieces are incredible with such artistry. The pieces are sold and shipped worldwide and from the appearance of the factory and shop, it is doing well.

The tour is led to another building owned by the factory shop and it is a magnificent restaurant where we eat a delicious lunch.

After lunch, we walk up the street to the Church of the Nativity which is still under reconstruction. Standing in line for a long time, we learn the Russian tour group is behind us and that they only come for one day and must catch a plane back home the same day. The Japanese tour group is in front of us as well as those of other nationalities and the line is not moving at all. Taking photos of the elaborate chandeliers and iconic displays helps some as we move ever so slowly toward the steps that lead down to the cave where Mary laid the Christ Child in the manager. Finally, the group begins to move faster and down the stairs. Since I had seen it in 2015, I moved quickly to allow those who had never been there to see the caves.

Parked under the Bethlehem Mall, we boarded the buses for Jerusalem, our home away from home and stopped by the Bible Lands Museum. We spent time studying the model of ancient Jerusalem and the temple that stood on the Temple Mount. The model is on a gigantic scale and has a model of the Roman barracks, homes, and the walls. Standing on the second floor near the railing, one can see the entire model and city in detail and the guide used a laser pointer to point out specific places that are of interest on the model. Inside the Bible Lands Museum were many interesting artifacts and ancient pieces of the history of Israel.

CHAPTER 14

His Peace

And Moses went up from the plains of Moab unto the mountain of Nebo, to the top of Pisgah, that is over against Jericho. And the LORD shewed him all the land of Gilead, unto Dan, And all Naphtali, and the land of Ephraim, and Manasseh, and all the land of Judah, unto the utmost sea, And the south, and the plain of the valley of Jericho, the city of palm trees, unto Zoar. And the LORD said unto him, This is the land which I sware unto Abraham, unto Isaac, and unto Jacob, saying, I will give it unto thy seed: I have caused thee to see it with thine eyes, but thou shalt not go over thither.
(Deuteronomy 34:1-4)

The guide meets the tour group in the lobby of the hotel and announced the plans for the day included Masada, Qumran, Jericho, the Dead Sea, and camel rides. Everyone was excited to begin the adventure. The buses took us through barren desert with scarce shrubs beside the Dead Sea. Mountains were on one side; the sea on the other along the highway. One mountain is distinct from the others and that one is Masada.

Herod's castle on the side of the mountain can be seen by looking over the side. There two bathhouses or *mikvehs* with elaborate tiles for ritual bathing were located there. Arched doorways led into lavishly tiled rooms. It was amazing to see what ancient people actually lived like here. Then after many sites are examined, we look down the ramp built by the Romans and at the piles of large round stones that were unused ammunition. Only two women and five children are said to have survived by hiding in a cistern on the mountain to tell the story of what happened to the other people there. We leave Masada on the cable cars and make our way back onto the highway to Qumran.

At Qumran, the guide pointed out the caves where the Dead Sea Scrolls were found and gives a description of all the features of the ancient buildings there. In view from excavations were ancient ritual baths, building foundations, and walls. Rooms thought to be where the Dead Sea Scrolls were copied were noted. We did not see the movie of how they were found like we did in 2015 nor did we eat in the restaurant there. Loading the buses, the drivers drove toward Jericho.

Along the highway, the guide points out a large building with a high fence around it as a prison and on the opposite side of the highway, a hotel. In the center of the city is a traffic circle that has not been finished. The traffic circle has a fisted hand with a shahada finger pointing upward with a new moon icon stuck in the tip of the finger with a round sign on the side that reads, "Jericho City of the Moon". Blue graffiti covered the sign and an old power drill or jack hammer lay idle on the dirt ground around it. The bus passed by elaborate mansions surrounded by walls that the guide said belonged to the sultans of Jericho. We had lunch at the Sultana Restaurant and Cafe.

After lunch, the group arrived at Tel Jericho or ancient Jericho. Jericho was a large and thriving city for centuries before the exodus from Egypt. In fact, Jericho is one of the oldest cities in the world as is stated by a sign at its entrance. Near the entrance is a water spring called Elisha's Fountain.

> And he went forth unto the spring of the waters, and cast the salt in there, and said, Thus saith the LORD, I have healed these waters; there shall not be from thence any more death or barren land. So the waters were healed unto this day, according to the saying of Elisha which he spake.
>
> 2 Kings 2:21-22

Jericho is located near the Jordan and seventeen miles south of Jerusalem. It has a warm climate in winter and hot in summer as it was this day. The heat shimmered as we walked up steps to the top of the Tel to a covered pavilion but being the last of the group, we sat on the outside in the sun. The pastor read the scriptures on Jesus' temptation in the wilderness from Matthew 4. The pastor noted that regardless of who you are, temptation will come! However; temptation can be overcome through prayer. It can be conquered.

> And Jesus being full of the Holy Ghost returned from Jordan, and was led by the Spirit into the wilderness, being forty days tempted of the devil. And in those days he did eat nothing: and when they were ended, he afterward hungered.
>
> Luke 4:1-2

Jesus was tempted for forty days and after that became hungry. It is not a sin to be tempted as long as nothing happens but don't be surprised or fooled by temptation when it comes. It can come in unexpected times and events so be careful.

After prayer, the guide pointed out the ancient city walls that had been excavated and the walls that dated from Joshua's time. There were wells and pieces of walls all around the Tel Jericho. Joshua sent spies to survey the land and the city of ancient Jericho. The Bible tells us that Rahab the harlot took the spies in and later helped them escape. For her help, she and her family were spared when Israel destroyed the city (Joshua 2:1, Joshua 6:1). The fall of the city occurred after the Israelites marched around it blowing trumpets, once a day for six days and then seven times on the seventh day. Then, as the priests blew the trumpets, the people shouted and the walls fell.

Back on the buses, our guide stops the bus, gets off at a sidewalk store and brings back a huge bunch of Judean bananas still on a stem. He broke off two bananas each and gave them to us. The bananas had a deeper, woody flavor and not as sweet as those in supermarkets here, but they were delicious. Sidewalk stores or vendors had all kinds of fruits, vegetables, eggs and breads for sale near the street in Jericho. God is so good!

The guide pointed out the sycomore tree that in Luke's gospel, little Zacchaeus resorted to climbing in order to get a better view of Jesus in Jericho. (Luke 19:4) The *ficus sycomorus* species of fig is most exclusively called a *sycomore* and is not the American sycamore. According to the guide, this tree has been around since the time of Jesus. It is a huge tree.

Leaving Jericho, the bus departed for the Dead Sea and those who wish to swim or float in it may do so. The people in this swimming area are mostly Muslim and the fellow at the gate did not want to allow me passage, except the pastor's wife intervened and pulled me through and told him that I was with her. I had my cross necklace on and did not attempt to hide it. Many chose to sit and eat ice cream due to the walk down the hill to the sea. This site was different from last year's site in that the entire area was covered with green outdoor carpet and was richly decorated. The view of the sea and the surrounding mountains was the most outstanding of its features.

The bus stopped near a roadside stand where camel rides were going on and anyone wishing to ride a camel could ride a camel. Almost all the group rode the camels except for my sister, another lady, and I. We took photos from the bus and were entertained by everyone's antics.

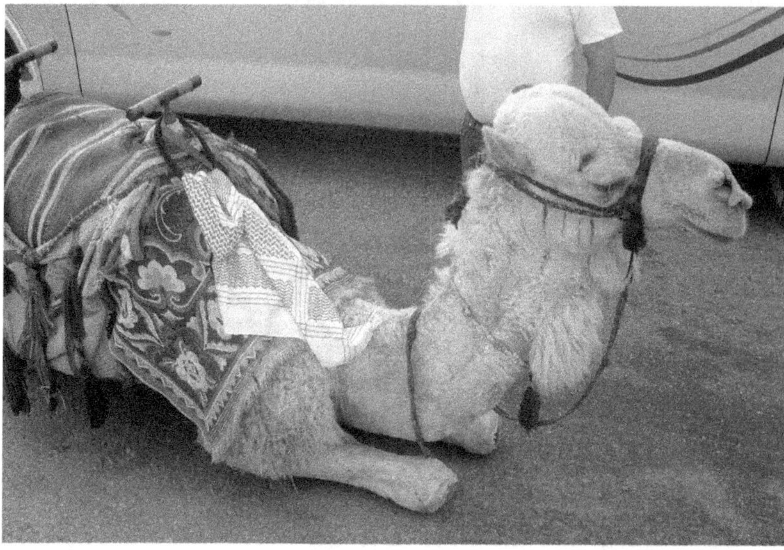

CHAPTER 15

He is Alive!

"But now is Christ risen from the dead,
and become the firstfruits of them that slept."
(1 Corinthians 15:20)

Last day in Israel! It seemed the time has flown by on gossamer wings. The guide informed us that we had a busy schedule ahead. After a most delicious breakfast, we were taken to the Garden Tomb where we see an empty tomb.

> And the angel answered and said unto the women, Fear not ye: for I know that ye seek Jesus, which was crucified. He is not here: for he is risen, as he said. Come, see the place where the Lord lay.
>
> Matthew 28:5-6

Moving on we go to the Mount of Olives and down a steep road beside the cemetery to Gethsemane and the Church of All Nations. After a brief visit to these, the bus takes us up a street to the Western Wailing Wall where we walk to the wall and those who wish to can pray or place prayers. Then we headed back to the bus and to the top of Mount Zion to the Church of Gallicantu or St. Peter's Church. Inside the church, the guide points out the murals on the walls depicting Peter and Jesus and how Peter would deny him three times.

> But Peter said unto him, Although all shall be offended, yet will not I. And Jesus saith unto him, Verily I say unto thee, That this day, even in this night, before the cock crow twice, thou shalt deny me thrice.
>
> Mark 14:29-30

Under the church are the tiny cave rooms where the apostles met to have church.

After this site, lunch was served in the American Embassy located on a street around the Mount of Olives. Back in Jerusalem, we began to walk the Via Dolorosa at St. Anne's Church or the site of the Last Supper and Day of Pentecost. The Japanese tour group was in front of us and sang "Alleluia." It was beautiful and God's presence filled the church as a wind blew through it. Praise the Lord! Hallelujah!

Moving slowly in our group, we followed all the stations on the Via Dolorosa to the final destination in the Church of the Holy Sepulchre. There we follow the guide up the narrow stairs to the second-floor room and to my shock and surprise, everything had changed. There were no stone paths and no cul-de-sac of stone behind a metal rail. There was a level flat floor with carpet covering it entirely! A nun sat on a bench where the wall would have been and a huge wooden armoire or chest sat against the wall where the cul-de-sac had been only one year before. The room could have been a living room in a house! The entire place looked totally different!

The guide was looking at me strangely as I walked around dazed that I remembered nothing of this place except the chandelier lights and the altar were the same. I did not remember being in the first room at all. I got into line to go to the altar but by the time I got almost to it, everyone else in our group had gone. I bypassed the altar and noticed a brown-robed priest sitting in a chair past the altar looking at me. That area, too, had changed.

I remembered a worn stone path with rose bushes beside it. A nun was sitting on the bench reading a book near the front at the stairs. The bench was not there in 2015. Bewildered and confused at what I had seen, I went down the stairs like I had in 2015. Even the stairs seemed to have changed. There were more of them at the bottom and it looked like the floor had been torn up and removed making a long reach to the floor. The walls were dark gray and I turned right like I did in 2015, but the walls were not bright and yellow as they had been then, but were dark gray and dreary like a basement.

Instead of going straight back past the broken stone of Adam's Chapel, they went on and on like a dark cavern with very little lighting and did not end like I remembered but continued around in a dark, dank place. The whole wall with the white broken stone was now a small enclosed stone over a man's head high on the wall. Stunned, I told the Holy Spirit that He

I had no idea where I was going or what had happened to the place; it was so different. I turned around and went back to the front of the church and joined the rest of the group who were waiting to see the tomb. However, the Japanese tour group were in line first and they were going two at a time into the tomb, so the guide told us about the tomb and then we all walked around the Edicule. Once again, I was shocked to see the floor was in horrible shape except some of it had been replaced with new tiles while others were coming apart and peeling up.

A couple of months after this trip, I saw an article that said the Church of the Holy Sepulchre was being renovated and lots of rocks were being removed from the church. They were redoing floors and walls and making a new structure for the Edicule. Not as interesting as it was in 2015, but what a relief that they had changed it during reconstruction!

The guide led the group back to the buses and we learned our departure would be at ten o'clock the next morning on Sunday. We were to be packed and ready for the rest of the tour to Rome, Italy.

CHAPTER 16

His Presence in Rome, Italy

But Paul said unto them, They have beaten us openly uncondemned, being Romans, and have cast us into prison; and now do they thrust us out privily? nay verily; but let them come themselves and fetch us out.
(Acts 16:37)

With the entire group loading the same Atalia airplane this time, we were not alone. After about four hours, we arrived in Rome and had to gather our luggage to take it to the tour buses and then on to the Cicerone Hotel. Rome was interesting to say the least. The streets were extremely busy with tiny cars, motorcycles, buses, and trucks. Horns honked and sirens screamed. There were modern streets and ancient walls. High-priced stores and kiosks selling clothing lined the streets and bazaars were everywhere on the side streets with everything imaginable to sell. It was a very busy city! After a dinner of pasta, we retired to our rooms to rest up for the next day.

Rome, Italy

Our new guide, an Italian, said he could out walk us all, so please keep up with him. We took the bus across the Tiber River, the third longest in Italy that runs through Rome. Rome was founded on the banks of the Tiber in the year 753 BC, according to the guide. The guide pointed out landmarks like a huge castle and a pyramid on our way to Saint Paul's Basilica. It was so enormous that we could see it even before we arrived there. It was an amazing structure of huge columns and figures that appeared to be glowing with a cross on the very top of the pinnacle. Upon arrival, we were body-scanned by the military just like at the airport. They said it was because of vandalism to some of the sites. The inside of the portico had huge columns, elaborate gold ceilings, frescos, marble floor tiles, murals and round gold framed photos of all the popes from Saint Peter and Saint Paul to the present-day pope, Saint Francis. Only Saint Francis had a light on it while the others were darkened. Acts 28:16-20 was scripture that pertained to this place where they show a rock with a chain attached to two hooks because supposedly this is the place where Paul was chained. No one is allowed to touch the chain or rock, but the group could look over the side railing and take photos of it. What a monument to the legacy of Apostle Paul! His books in the New Testament and conversion story are an even greater legacy to him.

After leaving the cathedral, we drove by the American Embassy in Rome and saw a huge yellow building with the American flag on it. We rode past ancient structures and listen to the guide's stories about them. He pointed out the angel on the side of the bridge going back over the Tiber River. We passed by balconies on buildings, churches with tall steeples, and horse and buggy rides. We walked down black cobblestone streets, go past gold framed windows with "Versace" on them, past police cars, and military on our way to the Trevi Fountain.

An aqueduct was constructed in 19 BC by Agrippa, the son-in-law of Emperor Augustus, to bring water from the Salone Springs about twenty-one miles away to Rome to supply this fountain. The Trevi Fountain was in Rome when Paul was there. Coming down steep stairs from the top street along the side of the fountain, I moved into a space on the balcony to take a side view photo of it.

Suddenly a policeman comes in beside me so fast that his gun pokes me in the ribs. He exuded a calming presence as he looked at me like time was standing still and then he looked over the side of the balcony and as I was done with my photo, I edged slowly away and down the steps bewildered at his actions because the nearest person to me was a young man about four feet away sitting on the wide concrete balcony. I didn't know if he was suspicious of me or the young man. Another angel watching over me, I guess! I joined the group to continue down the steps to the street where thousands of people were milling around in front of the fountain. We took photos from every angle and then went into a pizza shop to eat lunch.

We visited the Sistine Chapel and saw amazing murals, but we were not allowed to take photos in there due to the exposure of light on the tapestry wall hangings. There were statues lining every hall in all their glory.

Then we went on to Saint Peter's Basilica containing the *Pietà* by Michaelangelo Buonarroti and it was just as richly decorated as Saint Paul's had been with gold arches and ceilings, marble floors, and columns. There was a confessional that must have been created for a giant under a gold-dome ceiling and dead popes in glass coffins on display.

At the end of this seven-mile walk, the guide was still going strong, but the rest of us were ready for our rooms.

Our last full day in Rome began with a visit to the Coliseum. This place is humungous with stone block columns and overhead arches. On display are plaster cast heads that say they are the ancient people of Rome, some are female and some male. We walk to the top floor and around the balcony where in ancient times people sat and watched as caged animals in stalls under the floor were let up to kill Christians just for sport.

This place is so enormous that people opposite to us look like ants. Making our way back to the ground floor, we see cells with jail bars where the guide says that it was possible that Apostle Paul was held during his journey there. The group gathers at the bottom floor and walks together to the Titus' Arch Monument that is not very far from the Coliseum. It is gargantuan! On one side is a depiction of Titus' carrying away the Temple treasures from Jerusalem to Rome that includes the Golden Menorah. On the inside of the same column is Titus in his chariot driving the Jews ahead of him as slaves.

Not far from the Titus Monument is the Roman Appii Forum government seat that is mentioned in Acts 28. Ancient buildings are all around this area with tall columns standing alone like sentinels guarding buildings that are long past their prime. We walk on and come to Mamertinum Prison where Paul was kept until his trial. A sign in Italian states it is the prison of Apostle Peter and Paul. According to the fourth-century historian Eusebius, Apostle Paul was beheaded here in AD 67. Walking through the government seat, we pass huge statues of Marcus Aurelius on his horse and another of Pollux on his horse. Eventually, the end of the government complex is in sight with some interesting steps the guide says were designed by Da Vinci down to the street level where the buses are parked waiting for us. Our guide says his goodbyes because he has another group waiting for him to guide them. Back at the hotel, the group decides to go shopping and out to lunch. Some of us shop for awhile and then go to a street restaurant and dine al-fresco on margarita pizza and tiramisu at the Grotta Azzurra. It has been a sad, exciting, and wonderful day to be in Rome!

After a delicious continental breakfast in the hotel, good-byes are said, hugs are given and a limo came to take my sister, our friend, and me to the airport for the flight back to the USA. A storm caused some flights to be delayed, so we were forced to stay on the plane until well after dark before we could get off the plane in Atlanta. Rain poured and it took awhile to get onto the interstate to drive toward home. Finally, the weather got so bad that with prompting from Holy Spirit, I convinced my sister to let me rent a room for us to spend the night in Georgia. We arrived back a day late, but it was well worth the sunny drive the next day.

Lessons learned all around, be safe not sorry! God is with us! I listened to Jesus speaking through His Holy Spirit for He is my Rock in whom I put all my trust! Some people believe and think it was the Jews that killed Jesus while some think it was the Romans. But what did Jesus himself say?

> Then saith Pilate (Roman) unto him, Speak thou not unto me? know thou not that I have power to crucify thee, and have power to release thee? Jesus answered, Thou could have no power at all against me, except it were given thee

> from above: therefore he that delivered me unto thee hath the greater sin.
>
> John 19:10-11

Then in John 10:18-19, Jesus said,

> No man takes it from me, but I lay it down of myself. I have power to lay it down, and I have power to take it again. This commandment have I received of my Father. There was a division therefore again among the Jews for these sayings.

In the words of the prophet, Jeremiah,

> Ah, Lord GOD! Behold, You have made the heavens and the earth by Your great power and outstretched arm. There is nothing too hard for You. You show lovingkindness to thousands, and repay the iniquity of the fathers into the bosom of their children after them--the Great, the Mighty God, whose name is the LORD of hosts. You are great in counsel and mighty in work, for your eyes are open to all the ways of the sons of men, to give everyone according to his ways and according to the fruit of his doings.
>
> Jeremiah 32:17-19

CHAPTER 17

Praise Him!

"Let everything that hath breath praise the LORD."
(Psalm 150:6)

For Jesus, there was no other way to make a way to heaven and the Father except by way of the cross and *giving* His life for all to be saved. He proved many times that He could escape by becoming invisible to people. He could make people blind to His physical presence. He could make them forget what was happening and when it happened. He could change His appearance, His clothing (Luke 9:29) and He had the power to call forth legions of angels (Luke 26:53). His message is that He died for everyone Some people blame the Romans, Pilate, Herod and the Jews chief priests, and all the Jewish people for Jesus' crucifixion. It was God's perfect plan of salvation that made this event happen, and when He said it was finished, He meant it! He did not arise from the dead to blame anyone. Not the Jews, not the Romans not any of the people. Read the scriptures with new eyes and see. He is not among the dead but is truly living!

> Who is the image of the invisible God, the firstborn of every creature: For by him were all things created, that are in heaven, and that are in earth, visible and invisible, whether *they be* thrones, or dominions, or principalities, or powers: all things were created by him, and for him: And he is before all things, and by him all things consist.
>
> Colossians 1:15-17

It makes sense that Jesus can hide in plain sight from anyone at any time and in any form and any where. He can be in the visible world or the invisible parallel universe because there are no restrictions on Him. After His resurrection, Jesus appeared in another form to two of the disciples in Mark 16:12 "After that he appeared in another form unto two of them, as they walked, and went into the country." However; no one believed that He had when it was told to them. He appeared many times to them but many did not believe even though they saw Him as in John 21:14 and Luke 24:15. Luke says in verse 16 that their eyes were *holden* so they did not know him.

Holden appears to mean blinded in some way because they clearly did not see Him or recognize Him. He could appear and disappear and change His appearance as in these verses: Mark 16:9, 12; Luke 24:16, 31, 36-43; John 20:14-16, 19, 26; 21:4; Revelation 1:12-17; 10:1-3. In Luke 24:16, 31 and John 20:14-15, it seems that the people's eyes who saw Jesus were affected in some instances and in the other passages it seems He changed form when He did not appear normally, so that they would not know Him. Open your heart, open your spiritual eyes and you too will see Him. He is here, right now on this earth!

Jesus can go wherever He wants to go. The sun gets hotter as the music swells across the air waves so I get up and follow my sister to a shade on the side of the wall. This was a wonderful evening of praise by Matt and Laurie Crouch, Joel and Victoria Osteen and Christine Caine and Bethel Church. Praise Him who made us all!

The next day we sing praise on the tour bus as we go through the Jordan Valley which is green and growing with plants of every kind that is such a miracle because in 2016, it was brown everywhere. On the way to Nazareth, a car driven by a young woman rammed into the side of the tour bus under my window as the bus driver turned left for Nazareth and she attempted to pass the bus at the intersection. After sometime, the problem was cleared and the bus rolled on to Nazareth. After Nazareth, lunch was an open-air picnic at Megiddo with fellowshipping and peace. Then we went on to the event at Galilee.

At the Galilee, birds fly over the open amphitheater as a camera drone swoops in to snap photos of the crowd. The joy of the music and praise rings across the water as flocks of birds seem to dip and fly to the rhythm. Joseph Prince preaches and Christine Caine, Joel and Victoria Osteen, Matt and Lauric Crouch give us words of scripture and wisdom and praise. The crowd of diverse countries is boisterous and the music is loud. It is like a wonderful dream. It was announced that those wishing to be baptized in the Jordan River could do so the next day and many pastors were recruited to help baptize.

There was a night of communion at the Garden Tomb with the tour members spread throughout the Garden. The fellowship was so warm, His presence must have been there. We sat on chairs, benches, and anywhere there was a place to sit as sparkling grape juice and tiny crackers were passed to every person to enjoy the communion. What a glorious time!

In Caesarea, the evening sun illuminates the amphitheater in a bright glow of yellow and orange as the crowd of about 2,000 sings along with Bill Johnson and the Bethel Church singers in praise to the God of Israel. Flags of various countries are presented and a thunderous round of applause rings around the theater. A presentation of how Trinity Broadcasting Network was passed down to Matt was shown and it was a gentle reminder that the beloved Paul and Jan Crouch were with us only in spirit. Matt and Laurie Crouch, Joel and Victoria Osteen, Christine Caine, and Joseph Prince each preached and taught messages for all. As the light gave way to darkness and the sun dipped below the Mediterranean Sea, the praise swelled to a crescendo and moved with the Spirit. How awesome you are, LORD, maker of heaven and earth!

"According to thy name, O God, so *is* thy praise unto the ends of the earth: thy right hand is full of righteousness." (Psalm 48:10)

If you do not know Jesus Christ, you can be saved simply by saying this prayer, "Jesus, have mercy on me, a sinner. I believe that you are the Son of God and that you died for my sins. I believe you were born of the Virgin Mary and that you died on the cross and rose again as it is written in the Holy Bible. I am sorry for all the things that I have done that hurt others and you. Forgive me for all my sins. Come into my heart, Lord Jesus and take charge of my life. Make me what you would want me to be. Cleanse my heart of all sin. I confess you now as my Lord and Savior. Fill me with Your Holy Spirit and write my name in the Lamb's Book of Life so that I may see you and that I may live with you forever in heaven. In Jesus Christ's name I ask these things. Amen."

"Jesus said unto him, I am the way, the truth, and the life: no man comes unto the Father, but by me." (John 14:6)

Only Jesus can give you the freedom and peace and love that will fill your heart and soul. Only He can send the Holy Spirit, your Comforter from God. See Him! He is here!

Notes, Credits & Acknowledgements

Jamieson, Robert, A.R. Fausset, David Brown. [1884] *A Commentary: Critical, Experimental, and Practical on the Old and New Testaments*. Toledo, OH: Jerome B. Names & Co. (Page 2) Public Domain.

Youssef, Dr. Michael. Leading the Way, *The Best of Israel Tour 2015*. PO Box 20100 Atlanta, GA 30325-9877. 877-251-8294

Noseworthy Travel Services. NTS PO Box 6378, Lakeland, FL 33807, noseworthytravel.com/tours. nts@travelwithus.com. 1-800-929-4684.

Merritt, Dr. James. Touching Lives. 1800 Satellite Blvd. Duluth, GA 30097. *Israel and Rome Tour 2016*.

World Pilgrim Tours. 3473 Lawrenceville-Suwanee Rd #E, Suwanee, GA 30024. Worldpilgrimtours.com. 1-770-271-0110.

Crouch, Matt and Lorie. Osteen, Joel and Victoria. Prince, Joseph, Caine, Christine. Trinity Broadcasting Network. *Hope and Grace Tour 2018*. TBN PO Box A, Santa Ana, Calif. 92711, TBN.org, prayer@tbn.tv. 1-888-731-1000.

CPSIA information can be obtained
at www.ICGtesting.com
Printed in the USA
LVHW012001041119
636283LV00014B/1395

9 781640 886032